D1030037

How to Write a Speech

Books by Edward J. Hegarty

How to Write a Speech

by EDWARD J. HEGARTY

SALES CONSULTANT; FORMERLY DIRECTOR
OF SALES TRAINING
ELECTRICAL APPLIANCE DIVISION
WESTINGHOUSE ELECTRIC CORPORATION

McGraw-Hill Book Company, Inc.
New York   London   Toronto

HOW TO WRITE A SPEECH

FOURTEENTH PRINTING

27865

Published by the McGraw-Hill Book Company, Inc.

Printed in the United States of America

This book is dedicated to everyone who has ever been called upon to say a few words

Preface: Why—How to Write a Speech

Anybody can deliver a speech. Men prove that every day. They stand up on their feet, and they say what they want to say. If a man fears he can't make a speech, he can take a short course in public speaking and almost immediately he will acquire the ability to rise and give out with words of wisdom or what not.

But few men can write a speech. That's why you hear so many inept speeches. Go to church on Sunday, to your service club, your trade association, to any business meeting, and you hear speakers who have spent time and effort in preparing a speech. Yet they don't interest you. They talk loud enough. They have the voice, the presence, the words, but they don't know how to put those words together in a way to arouse your interest.

You hear a man make a speech for a cause in which you are interested, but the way the fellow puts the appeal just about breaks your heart. It isn't that he can't make a talk. He simply doesn't know how to make his talk interesting.

Then you hear a man who isn't a good talker, talking about a cause in which you have no interest. Yet he holds your interest for twenty or thirty minutes or an hour. His voice lacks volume; it squeaks; he has no presence—nothing to hold you but his message. Yet he holds your interest through the whole talk.

What is the difference? One knew how to write a speech—the other didn't.

Now most of the bad speeches you hear have good material. The speakers have put hours into assembling the data. Properly handled, this material could be made into an interesting talk. But these speakers just don't know how to handle speech material properly.

The suggestions in this book are assembled to give you a formula for writing a talk. It is a formula that good speakers use. It is one that will help you write a speech that audiences will like.

The ideas presented come from listening to speakers—not a few, but hundreds of them. They are the result of a busy notebook. I hear what the speaker says. I analyze the speech construction. I watch the speaker's stunt or his bit of audience participation. As each unfolds I note what he does and the effect on the audience. These effects are reported here. These pages explain how good speakers get effects with groups. It is my idea—naïve perhaps—that if the average speaker would follow the techniques of the successful speaker, audiences would applaud better speeches.

EDWARD J. HEGARTY

Contents

Introduction

I was sitting in the club car rolling out of Chicago bound for home, a six-hour ride ahead of me. I had just attended a meeting —four days of speeches and planned presentations. In the thirty-six talks there was one good speech—one that listeners would like—one in thirty-six—less than 3 per cent. That is not a good average. In those talks there was good material, plenty of it. Some men were working with material that could have made excellent speeches. The notebook that I leafed through as I sat on the train proved this fact. And I was surprised, too, at the notes I had taken, for I had never been much of a note taker. But in this case I had written notes and comments on each speech—what was wrong with it, what was right.

Before the meeting all the speakers had done a lot of work in preparing their presentations. And it was a shame to see all of their work wasted. Each person meant for his presentation to be good, of course. With the amount of work, each should have been good. Some of the men read their talks. It so happened that not one of them knew how to read a speech. Others talked with charts or other exhibits in a way that left much to be desired. Others just talked. But it so happened that out of thirty-six talks only one was good. Now why was that? Well, my conclusion as I analyzed my notes was this: These speakers didn't know how to write good speeches.

I turned the notebook over, started to write on the back of the pages the headings under which I could give advice on how to write a good speech. I tried to organize a formula which, if applied to all the talks I had heard, would have made every one of them good. When I reached home, which was a little over three hundred miles away, I had outlined twenty-six chapters for this book. I took that train ride three years ago. Since then I've been attending meetings, listening to speeches, making notes. I've been making speeches myself, cutting and trying. In these past three years a number of chapters have been added to the original outline, and a number checked out.

As I listen and make notes I have become convinced that the trouble with speeches is in the writing. Men who give speeches just don't know how to write scripts that are to be spoken. There's a difference between written language and spoken language—a big difference. Most speakers don't know this. There are certain rules to hold interest, but speakers seem to ignore them. There are rules to make dull material interesting; to a great army of speakers these are unknown. All of these rules are simple. Most good speakers follow them knowingly or unknowingly. Yet it's strange how few of the average speakers know them or remember them or put them to use.

In these pages I have attempted to put down those rules for that average speechmaker. Each chapter lists suggestions that will help the average speaker make his material more interesting to the audience that is going to hear it. So remember, this is written for the average speechmaker. The expert may get some suggestions from it, but the average man should profit most. This is a plan for organizing your material, for making it interesting, for getting it down on paper, and then for checking it. Then just for added measure, you might find some suggestions for using it. But the latter is not the purpose of this book. The purpose is to tell you how to write a speech. So let's get on with the telling.

How to Write a Speech

1. Get Off the High Horse

You're going to write a speech. And you're scared to death. Sure, I know you're not afraid of the speechmaking. Spouting it out is comparatively easy; in fact, it may be fun. But writing—ah! That is another story.

But relax, and let's talk about it. Push aside the paper and pencil, or if you are planning to dictate your speech, tell Miss What's-Her-Name to come back later. Somehow this invitation to make a speech puffs you up like a gas balloon. Why, I don't know. You're the same person you were before you took the phone call or read the letter. The ideas you will present to these people will be the same old two-by-two's that you've been giving the barber and the bartender. There is nothing startling or revolutionary about these ideas. Well, if you are the same person with the same ideas, what's the sense of getting puffed up?

So let's deflate and discuss why they asked you to make this speech. I don't mean what they told you in the invitation—let's go into the real why. Is it because Whosis is the program chairman, and he knows you or has heard of you? Or maybe somebody has asked your manager in Fort Worth, and he tried to think of somebody and sold you to them. Or perhaps they've got twenty-seven turndowns and in desperation they are grabbing at you. Most invitations are like that. So let's not get puffed up over the bid.

Then let's consider what they want. Well, they want you to talk for twenty or thirty minutes. They hope you will be good, but they have their fingers crossed. They want you to tell them something, or to sell them something, and they hope you'll do it in a lively, amusing, and interesting manner that keeps them awake. But they're not too hopeful. They have been stung again and again, and here they are stuck with you and they hope for the best.

Don't let any of the externals of this invitation confuse you. Perhaps they did ask for a biographical sketch and your photo. They told you they want to run them in the local newspapers, but don't let that fool you. They need the publicity to get a crowd at the meeting. Then, too, the chairman may have mentioned that little cocktail session before the meeting. But that, too, is custom.

So let's be cold in our analysis of this bid to you. Perhaps the picture is not too flattering, but it's the McCoy. I've been on both sides. I've been the committee, and I've been the guest speaker, and I know. I'm bringing it to you to deflate you, to puncture your pomposity, so that you'll get off the high horse. For I know that if I get you down to the realities at the start, I'll do you a big favor and I'll do your audience a big favor.

Why do I bother to blot out this picture you have of yourself as a guest speaker? Well, I've done a lot of ghostwriting—putting together speeches for others to give. An associate asks you to write a speech for him. You discuss the subject matter, the occasion, the group, and you write it. You bring it in, and he reads it, slowly, carefully. Then he clears his throat. "This is good, but I wonder if it has the dignity I should have in addressing this group?"

You feel like saying "Nuts," but he's the boss, or an associate you don't want to offend. You realize that he's not considering this speech as he should. That he's pouted up like a pigeon and he won't be happy until he has added to the script a number of dignified words, preferably those of seven letters, words which are not his, which he may have trouble pronouncing and with which he isn't too familiar.

I'm sure you have heard the story of the toastmaster who introduced the speaker of the evening. He told about the wonderful scholastic and business record of the speaker, he covered the man's history back to his boyhood, he mentioned his fine mother and his Christian upbringing, he pictured himself as a boyhood friend of the speaker, and then he turned to the man sitting next to him and whispered, "What's this guy's name, anyway?"

And yet many times when you deliver a speech you have written yourself, the fellow who knows you, the boy who grew up with you, your best pal, your closest companion, your buddy asks that same question, "Who is this guy, anyway?" And they go further than that. They wonder also, "How does he get that way?" "Who does he think he is?"

Now in making a good speech, I want you to think of you as yourself. Not someone else in your Sunday suit, with your smile, up there playing a part, trying to impress the audience with his erudition or to confound it with his wisdom. I want you to think of you as yourself—a regular guy, sounding off before a group of regular guys.

Let's start with that premise. We're not going to step out of character for an instant. We're going to write a talk in the most natural way we know. We're not going to dress up our remarks in Sunday language. We're not going to try to make an impression. We'll concentrate on getting over our message in an interesting way.

Always when you set out to prepare a speech, your first obstacle is to get yourself off the high horse and down to earth. So take a deep breath, relax, and I'll tell you how to write a good speech.

2. Write a Synopsis

The first thing to do about your speech is to write a synopsis. Don't start on what the speechmakers call "the first draft." Write yourself a note explaining what you are trying to do with this speech, and then put down on paper an outline of how you are going to do the job.

What do I mean by a synopsis? Here's a formula.

1. A statement of your purpose or objective. What are you trying to do in this talk—to amuse, to instruct, to sell an idea? Write it down.
2. A statement of the philosophy of the talk. What will the group get out of it? Why is it to their benefit to listen to it? Write that out.
3. An outline of the points that you will cover in making the talk. These should be directed at your objective and should be in line with your philosophy.
4. A short summation of the points that you will leave with them. Remember that they can't remember a long list of points. Make this list short—three or four are about right.

The first part of the synopsis should be a statement of purpose. What is your purpose? To help old Charlie, who has been stuck with this meeting and needs a speaker? No, not that one. Is it to inform, to entertain, to persuade? Perhaps it's a bit of all those things. But write out that purpose—get down on paper what you are trying to do.

Now that is difficult. It is easier to start writing. But you will save time and effort if you clarify your purpose in a sentence or

4

two or three. How do you write that purpose? Well, let's illustrate.
I have a speech, a hardy perennial that has stood the test of hot
nights in smoke-filled rooms. The speech is called "How to Run a
Sales Meeting." I have done it fifty to sixty times before groups of
22 to 1500. Never yet has it failed me. So let's use it as an example.
Here is how the purpose of that speech could be written.

> PURPOSE—This speech is to be given to sales, sales promotion, and
> advertising managers. It will give them suggestions as to how to
> run better sales meetings. It will explain what a meeting is and give
> suggestions on room arrangement, talks, use of visual aids, timing,
> how to avoid the common mistakes, and how to build a good
> ending.

Note that I have described the audience in that first paragraph.
That's helpful. I do this same speech for general audiences and I
have to change certain illustrations which are quite familiar to sales
groups but might be confusing to a general audience.

As you read that paragraph describing the purpose of this speech
you can see that such a statement of your objective will help keep
you on the track. So first in this synopsis comes a statement of
purpose.

Next I try to write out a paragraph that states the philosophy of
the talk. This is my analysis of what warrants my audience listening
to me for ten, twenty, or thirty minutes. I try to put down what
they will get out of it.

> PHILOSOPHY—Most of the training of salesmen is done in sales
> meetings. If my suggestions will help these men put on better sales
> meetings, the salesmen of their companies will be better trained.
> If the salesmen are better trained, they will sell more manufactured
> goods and so more employees will be kept working in the factories.

With the purpose and the philosophy down on paper, my own
thinking is clarified. Now comes the third part of the synopsis—
listing the points to be covered. My procedure is to put down first
the headings of the subjects. Then under each heading I list points
that might be covered under that heading. In doing this don't
worry about wording or the order of the points.

Pick up the tube of that dictating machine, call in Miss What's-Her-Name, or get a piece of paper and a pencil. Then start dictating or writing.

The man told you what they wanted you to talk about, or you suggested a subject. He told you how much time you had. OK, that's enough. Dictate or write all the ideas you have on the subject as quickly as you can. Don't worry about having too little or too much. Put down in a hurry everything you think of.

Why fast? Well, if you stop to think, you are lost. Don't consider whether or not you will say this or that or can say this or that, or whether or not the boss will approve. That's what makes speech writing such a chore for most persons. They put down an idea and then scratch it out. That leaves them exactly where they started. So do this fast. What you want is a list of ideas that you might use. When you have it all down you can go back and revise. To show you what I mean I will write out the synopsis of the talk, "How to Run a Sales Meeting." Because this talk has been done a number of times, the synopsis might be more finished than your first try. First we need a sheet of paper, then a headline like this:

SYNOPSIS OF TALK—HOW TO RUN A SALES MEETING

PURPOSE—This speech is to be given to sales, sales promotion, and advertising managers. It will give them some suggestions as to how to run better sales meetings. It will explain what a meeting is and give suggestions on room arrangement, talks, use of visual aids, timing, on how to avoid common mistakes, and on how to build a good ending.

PHILOSOPHY—Most of the training of salesmen is done in sales meetings. If my suggestions will help these persons put on better sales meetings, the salesmen of their companies will be better trained. If salesmen are better trained, the salesmen will sell more manufactured goods and so more employees will be kept working in the factories.

OUTLINE—Now comes the outline. What are the points to be covered in this talk? Here are the headings with a short explanation of what is to be covered under each heading.

1. *Definition*—What a sales meeting is—a group sale. Make one talk or presentation and you sell a group. Not a mechanical job —a mental one. Most meetings are dull because men think of them as a mechanical job—Joe does this, Pete does this, and so on.

2. *Setting up the Room*—Selecting the room, what to try for, the theater arrangement, back to the wall, the entrance back of the audience, elevator story, chairs facing away from the windows, Pittsburgh story, no assistant behind you, get out the chairman, St. Paul story, man trying to light pipe with cigarette lighter, Milwaukee story, the head table—move it out.

3. *Variety*—Why they should try for variety—the vaudeville show, ball of fire, pail of water—the fallacy of saying our meetings have to be pretty much alike, the meeting-a-day-for-thirty-days example. Keep them awake with variety.

4. *Holding Interest with the Talk*—What to put in the talk to make it interesting. The anecdote, gossip, news, people, language, dramatizing what you say.

5. *Audience Participation*—We like to sing in the movies, a show of hands, getting them to say something, the advantage of having them repeat, why your instructions should be specific, the exercise, the roaster story.

6. *Don't Compete with Anything*—Why they shouldn't compete with anything when they talk—a waiter in the hotel dining room, the secretary to the boss, the outside disturbances, those inside the hall, how to handle both. The competition that the speaker sets up for himself, the product he passes out to the audience, the printed matter, the assistant working in the audience.

7. *Using Charts*—The janitor story, keep them covered, watch your position when talking from them, get enough light, spotlight, standing with a spotlight, don't study them, vary the introduction, practice using them.

8. *Fumbling*—Why the leader in the meeting should always be an expert, some examples, fumbling with notes, mention of time, admitting you don't know, depreciating, apologizing, hunting for props, handling yourself, small fellow reaching, suspenders, spectacles either on or off, practice using anything, leaning on lectern-table.

9. *Don't Rely on Humorous Stories*—Why the funny story is not too good for the sales meeting. How stories can be used, to get the audience relaxed, the Marsh story. Experience with small boy telling stories, memorize and rehearse, use of story to make a point, the three-story plan that will get laughs.

10. *End in High*—Most meetings seem to piddle out. The story of the man without an idea called upon by the chairman, what to do in such a case, the three-step ending, planning the end first.

THE SUMMATION—Now comes the summing up. What three or four points will you cover in the ending? In this talk these tie in with what has gone before. They are:

1. Salesmen are trained in sales meetings.
2. Better meetings mean better trained salesmen.
3. Better trained salesmen mean more sales.

As you look over this synopsis you may see how it can help you in writing your speech. My thought is that as you get down on paper some ideas of what you are to say, other ideas come to you. By organizing the subject under headings, you can write down any new idea that pops up under the heading to which it belongs. Usually you have some time to think about your speech, and it is a good idea to jot down any idea that comes to you. Write it on a piece of paper and then transfer it to the outline under the proper heading. It is through these additions that your speech takes on life. A taxi driver says something, your secretary lets off with a word of wisdom, there's an item in the news—any or all may be speech material. Fail to make notes and they are lost to the world, to you, and to your speech.

Please remember that the synopsis is only the start. Your first attempt doesn't need to be complete. Get down what you can think of now, and you will be surprised at how the subject matter will grow. You won't need padding; you'll be throwing away before you are finished.

In your first attempt the headings may not be in the final order. A study of the material available under each heading will help determine the order. Under certain ones you will have better speech material than under others. When you have analyzed the material you have, you may want to shift the headings so that the interest will be spread more evenly all through the speech. Let's say one part of the subject has little live-speech material in it. Then that part might be sandwiched in between two live parts.

In this talk, "How to Run a Sales Meeting," I have experimented with changing the parts. One change I tried was to reverse the last two parts, do the "End in High" sequence, and then follow with the "Don't Rely on Humorous Stories." My thinking was that this last sequence, in which I demonstrate how to tell funny stories to get laughs, would be a better ending. After two attempts I went back to the order given in the synopsis.

But let's examine those headings again.

1. The definition
2. Setting up the room
3. Variety
4. Interest them
5. Audience participation
6. Don't compete with anything
7. Using charts
8. Fumbling
9. Don't rely on humorous stories
10. End in high

As you look over the list, it is easy to see that except for 1, 2, 9, and 10, the remainder could be placed in almost any order. And that is what happened in the original organization of the speech. It is the same with the speech you are writing. If you shuffle the elements nobody but you will know that the shuffling has been done.

As you work on the talk there will probably be more change in the outline than in the purpose, the philosophy, or the summation, but as you continue these may change some too. By writing yourself a note in the synopsis, by telling yourself what you are going to do, how you are going to do it, and what you hope to accomplish, you save yourself time.

So you write a synopsis. And what do you include in it?

1. Your purpose or objective.
2. A statement of the philosophy of the talk.
3. An outline of the points that you will cover in reaching that objective.
4. A short summation of the points that you will leave with them.

But you don't get into the real job of organizing this opus until you tackle the next step in this process. So let's get on with that.

3. Lay It Out on Paper

Now that we have a synopsis, the next step is to lay out the speech on paper. Let's put it on one sheet where we can look at all of it at one time. It is difficult to consider the parts of a talk when they are on different sheets of paper, but when the parts are on one sheet, you can look, analyze, consider, and shift around to your heart's content. Just take a sheet of ordinary-size letter paper and mark it off in squares. I usually use a larger piece of paper so that I will have larger squares and can write more on each one.

The illustration below shows how such a layout will look when you have the paper squared off and have written the notes from your synopsis on the squares. Since this is a how-to talk, the subjects can be handled in almost any order; they have been marked on the sheet in the order given in the synopsis. The numbers in the upper right-hand corners of the squares indicate the order in which the subjects were listed in the synopsis.

With the subjects so laid out you can check for complete coverage. Have you listed all the points that should be covered? If not, what points should be brought in? Write these in one of the spare squares and indicate by arrows where they belong in the talk.

After I had studied the material shown on the layout on the following page, the order was changed to the order indicated by the numbers in the upper left-hand corners of the squares. This shift in sequence was made because some of the parts had better speech material than others, and the shift scattered the high points throughout the talk.

"What about logical order?" you ask. I'm trying to tell you how

OUTLINE—HOW TO RUN A SALES MEETING

1 DEFINITION ①	2 THE ROOM ②	3 VARIETY ③	4 INTEREST ④
What it is Group sale Mechanical vs. mental	Selecting room Theatre arrangement Entrance — Milwaukee Chairs Assistant Chairman—St. Paul Head table	Vaudeville Ball of fire Pail of water Meetings too much alike 30 days of meetings Keep awake	The story–Cleveland Gossip–Winchell News–vitamized cooking Language–proverbs Dramatizing People Indian story
7 AUDIENCE ⑤	8 COMPETITION ⑥	6 CHARTS ⑦	5 FUMBLING ⑧
Singing–Show of hands—Greeting Repeating a slogan Specific instructions Exercises to awaken them◄ The rooster story	Secretary–Waiter Boston story Assistant–Outside the band—The disturbances—Long Branch story Printed matter Samples	Janitor Covered–Position Light–Spotlight Canton story Studying–Vary the introduction–This is supposed to show Practice	Expert–notes–ms– cards–charts. Time–Depreciating Apologizing Suspenders Spectacles Leaning on lectern Hunting–Baltimore story–Practice
9 HUMOR ⑨	10 END ⑩		
Why the funny story is no good Use of story–Relax the audience or speaker Small boy story Memorizing Practice the 3 story idea	Don't let it die out. Recess before end Write end first Story of man called on without idea 3 step ending finally in conclusion	1. Train men to put on better mtgs. 2. You'll have better salesmen who sell more goods 3. You'll keep more men working in your factory	

to write an interesting speech—with the points in the order that will make the best speech. The trouble with most speeches is that the high points are bunched at one place and are followed by a long stretch of dead material. The usual practice is to throw the high points at the audience, one, two, three, four; then the lesser points; and finally the and-so-forths. The elements may be arranged in the logical order of importance, but I'm sure you'll agree that if you reversed the order, started with the and-so-forths, and wound up with the high points, you'd make a better speech.

My plan is to arrange these highs and lows so that you have good speech material on every page of the manuscript. In a good talk you want some new development at least every two or three minutes. Such organization helps hold attention for you. While you can't do all your organizing when you first lay out your talk on paper, you can get some of the work started.

As you look at the layout plan, you may ask, "If you are going to do this, why write a synopsis?" That is a good question. At times, if I know the audience and the subject, I start with the layout. The synopsis is simply an outline in another form that helps me get my philosophy of the speech on paper. When I do both, I give more thought to the subject, for it is natural that in going over the material twice I get down more ideas. You will note, too, if you care to check the synopsis against the outline, that as I went over the material the second time I added thoughts, ideas, and suggestions.

The illustration shows a rather clean sheet. My outlines are not at all like that. Usually my squares are about half the size of the pages of this book. When I write the headline, I do it in rather large letters, but the notes are scribbled in small script and they may run from one square into the next. Many times when I record a note I have an idea as to how that point should be expressed and I write the idea out too. If a suggestion for an anecdote to illustrate an idea comes to me, that suggestion goes down on paper too. The shifting of units which I handled so neatly by numbers in this illustration for reproduction purposes is usually handled by arrows. An arrow picks up square number 10 and places it between 3 and 4. The arrow that takes the story from square 10 to the next one illustrates my technique. I still have the speech before me, divided into its elements. I still can study it, but it is not the neat diagram shown in the illustration.

A layout also helps you to time your speech. You know how much time you will have and you know the relative importance of each point. Let's say you can speak at the rate of 125 words per minute. Then you'll speak 3,750 words in a thirty-minute talk. Now divide those words among your subjects according to the importance of each subject, and you have an idea of how long you can talk on each.

Time allotment brings up another point—what is to be left out. Perhaps a subject that you should cover cannot be handled in the time available for it. This forces a decision on whether or not to give the subject the once-over-lightly treatment or to leave it out altogether.

Such an outline helps you remember your speech. In the part on Variety, let's say there are four points to make. Now it is fairly easy to remember four points and the order in which they come. Thus, if I am thrown off the main track, I can come back much easier. I had four points in the beginning. When I went astray I had covered three. Point four is—thus I get back on the track.

One fellow I know builds his little squares into a bridge. "If I get off the track," he says, "I can always come back to my bridge." That is useful in any speech you make. Many times a snatch of conversation before you get up to talk, a question, or some audience reaction will send you off on a diversion not written into your speech. The outline should help you get back on the bridge at about where you went off.

The outline also helps you build up to the end. You don't want your speech to dwindle away to nothing. The outline lets you check to make sure that some meat and potatoes have been saved for the end. Let's arrange the elements so that we have something more than a few and-so-forths before we sit down. Always we need a good end; the layout should help us get it.

Laying out the talk on paper helps in these ways:

1. The outline gives you an opportunity to look at the speech all at once in the same way that an engineer might look at a finished drawing of his completed bridge.
2. It indicates where you might need additional material.
3. It indicates whether or not your high points bunch up.

4. It gives you an opportunity to go over your material a second time.
5. It allows you to shuffle the elements to spread interest all through the talk.
6. It helps in organizing your material to sell your idea or plan.
7. It allows you to check for complete coverage—have you covered all points?
8. It will help in your timing, in the amount of time assigned to each subject.
9. It permits you to check the order of the points and to put them in the proper place.
10. It helps you remember your speech.

4. Now You Need a Plan of Presentation

Now that you have the talk laid out on paper, you need a plan of presentation. One talk might be to inform, another to amuse, still another to appeal for some sort of action. Perhaps you never thought of it, but your plan of presentation in each case might be different. And no matter what your objective, you want to use the plan that applies to the speech you are going to do.

Perhaps you have seen a street peddler selling an exerciser. He is a short, stocky man with bulging muscles and has the husky voice of a man who has worked outdoors in all kinds of weather. He stands stripped to the waist in wintry weather, stretching a heavy belt of elastic material. Now he pulls it wide in front of him, now over his head, now behind him. As he goes through the exercises he tells his story to you. Does he tell you how the belt is made? Does he tell you how much strength it takes to pull it? Does he talk about the metal grips that fit the hands, about the quality of rubber, or the careful double stitching that holds it together?

Not so you can hear it. Instead he talks about you. Look at you, a skinny excuse for a man, underfed, undernourished, wrapped in a heavy overcoat while he stands there with no coat at all, not even an undershirt. Look at you, a puny, shrinking 36, while he's a 44 with a husky, he-man chest expansion.

As you listen to this kind of talk you begin to believe. You feel weak. You feel pains. You walked up to that street corner with a spring in your step. Now you don't feel too well. He extolls his beautiful sun tan and asks you to look at the people around you.

Instinctively, you glance at the fellow next to you. You see a pale face that matches yours.

You ask yourself, "Do I look as bad as that fellow?" The thought is hardly formed when someone steps up and hands over two dollars for the exerciser. Then another, then another. You put your hand in your pocket. Out comes your two dollars. You step up, you hand it to the man. You ask, "Are the directions inside?" Tarzan assures you that they are as he takes other dollars and hands over more packages.

Now that fellow uses a plan. He follows a formula that you can use in a talk that appeals for action. As I analyze his spiel, he follows four steps.

First, he makes you dissatisfied with the status quo. You are a weakling. You are letting yourself go. Soon you will be a wreck.

Second, he suggests a remedy. A strip of stretching rubber that can be used as an exerciser in the living room, the back yard, the cellar, or attic.

Third, he answers your questions and objections. He shows you how to use it. He demonstrates. He explains how you can start yourself on a new life, a life of fresh air, vim and vigor, and joy of being alive. He explains how you can build yourself into an Adonis —radiating health, how the girls will turn to look at you.

Fourth, he asks for action. He asks you to step up and hand over two dollars—the price of one good lunch—for this ticket to a better life.

There are just four steps to that formula, but if you want the audience to do something for you, there is no better plan. Here it is:

1. Make them dissatisfied.
2. Suggest a remedy.
3. Answer the questions and objections.
4. Ask for action.

That applies to the speech that attemps to plead for a cause. When your speech is to inform, the formula of the Negro preacher is fine. It runs:

First, I tells them what I's goin' to tell them.
Second, I tells them.
Third, I tells them what I done told them.

There are many of these speech formulas and you can find them
in books on public speaking. I urge you to select a formula that
you like. If you organize your speech on a formula it is much more
likely to start in the right direction and keep going in that direction
until it presents its message.

When you speak to an audience, the group sits there with a desire, a need, or a problem. Perhaps three or four or five of the group
have a strong interest in your subject matter. You know as you talk
that this small group is with you. But you must appeal also to the
other members of the group. What will they gain by being interested in this subject?

Perhaps they do not know they have a problem. Let's say they
all live in a small town. The town has a central square like the one
found in so many towns. All the traffic going through the town has
to go around that square. It costs the merchants much business and
many dollars each year. If your talk had to do with cutting the
main highway through the center of the square, you might have to
explain this problem to a large number of the audience.

If you are talking about a need, it may be one of which the group
is not aware. Perhaps they are members of a club, and with the
rising costs of running the club, the membership has to be increased
to keep the operation in the black. Not all members of the club
would know that. Many of them who use the facilities every day
may not be aware of the need for more members to keep the club
going. They like it as it is—uncrowded.

Or perhaps the club may have started a drive to make it the most
aggressive organization in town. That would be a desire of the
officers and the board of managers. The rank-and-file members
may not be aware of that desire.

If the members of your audience know that they have the need
or the desire, you have one speech problem. If they are not aware
of it, you must spend more time stating the problem or defining

the need or building up the desire. That means you must spend more time on the first steps of the exerciser salesman's formula. You must let them know there is a problem, and you must make them dissatisfied with things as they are.

Of course all speeches are not made to get audiences on some bandwagon. There are speeches that inform. You hear a man talk on color photography. He talks about his hobby, he shows some pictures, he answers some questions. If he is talking to camera bugs, he can talk about type of camera, lenses, filters, size of film, and other technical data. But if the audience does not know anything about taking pictures, he should confine himself to a description of his photographs. He should tell what the pictures are, where they were taken, what the persons in the pictures are doing. There are formulas for such speeches too.

When my boy was in high school he had some trouble with the themes he was required to write in English. I asked him how he wrote a theme. His answer was, "I just start to write and when I get enough words, that's it."

Many speech writers seem to have no more plan than that. I suggested to the boy that he use this formula:

1. What it is.
2. What it does.
3. How to use it.

Now that formula did not apply to all the themes he was asked to write, but it did give him a plan. And he confessed that that plan, simple as it was, helped him get a good mark in the course.

That formula—what it is, what it does, how to use it—is commonly used in describing a product or plan. It was not exactly right for all the boy's assignments, but by slightly changing the meaning of the steps he could plan a theme on almost anything. Further, if there were a choice in the assignment, he could select the subject to which the formula would apply. For a purely descriptive speech it is a good formula. Let's say you want to give a speech on the Black Fork: the shallow, muddy creek that runs under the stone bridge, which brings Route 36 into town. Here is how you might use that plan.

What it is: Describe the creek in all its unimpressive shabbiness. Today it is a disgrace. It invites the populace to dump trash in it. Talk about the tin cans and the broken beer bottles and the impression that it makes on travelers as they come into town—how they all say, "What kind of people could live in a town like this?"

What it does: Describe the good it does in carrying off the spring rains, and the bad, too, how it carries off the topsoil in the lowlands.

How to use it: Now tell how the creek could be made a thing of beauty; how a park could be made on its banks, with picnic benches and outdoor fireplaces, how the traveler would look at the little park and say, "What a pretty town."

The formula does not apply too well to this kind of subject, but notice that the notes above could be made into a good speech, one that would interest everybody in your town.

Another formula that might be used is the AIDA formula, well known in advertising and sales work. It goes:

1. Attract attention.
2. Arouse interest.
3. Create desire.
4. Suggest action.

It is a formula around which the advertising writer can build his advertisement, or the salesman can fashion his sale. Your assignment is similar when you make a speech that is designed to get the audience to do something you want done. So many pleas you hear have none of that persuasion in them. The speaker wants you to give—of your money or time—but he does not explain why you gain when you give.

Here is how that AIDA formula can be applied in a talk to office managers.

SUBJECT: FILTERED AIR

1. Attract attention   Gentlemen: If you could see your lungs right
                        now, what color do you think they would be?

Pink or dark red or maroon? Not at all. They would be black—black as the ace of spades.

2. Arouse interest

Why is that? Well, air has been passing through those lungs, and that air is loaded with dust. For in the end everything turns to dust—even you and I. Dust is the end of everything, of all solids. A beam of sunlight passing through a dark room is alive with moving particles. You see them floating about in the beam of light. But the ones you see are the big ones. There are perhaps a thousand times as many smaller ones that you can't see.

Look at the buildings in the city before and after sandblasting. That proves how much dirt and grime there is in the air. But try this. Your office is a clean place, isn't it? I am glad it is. Tomorrow morning run your finger along the top of the swinging door or the molding over the doorjamb. You'll see how much dust and grime there is in your life. Your fingers will be black, covered with the same kind of dust that blackens your lungs. Now, I am not criticizing the janitor in your offce. He can't keep those moldings clean. He would have to wipe them down every night to do it. So forget any idea of criticism. But let's think about how that dust got up on the molding. Nobody shoveled it up there. The air put it there. It is air-borne dust, the small particles that you can't see. The kind you breathe in every day. The kind that paints your lungs black. And paints the lungs of every one of your workers black.

You may say, "We have always had this dust and always will have it." That's true and it's a good thing, too, for dust has its good uses. Without dust there would be no rain. Each raindrop is built around a dust particle. The moisture condenses on the particle and falls to

2. Arouse interest
(*continued*)

the earth. Without the protection of dust in the atmosphere, the heat of the sun would be so intense that all life would be destroyed. Without dust, there would be no rain. Each the light and makes the sky look blue. Clouds would not form without dust. But dust is also a cause of disease, suffering, and death. Most communicable diseases of the respiratory tract are carried by dust. The so-called air-borne diseases are in reality dust-borne diseases.

Mother Nature knows this dust is harmful and tries to protect you against dust. Larger particles of dust are stopped by the hairs in the nose and the moist surfaces of the mucous membrane. The windpipe is also protected by countless cilia or tiny upright hairs which serve to sweep back into the upper throat any large particles that alight upon them. That dust in the air may give you any one of a number of diseases. For while you are protected by nature from the larger particles of dust, the smaller particles get by these defenses and when they reach the lungs they may do damage. For germs ride on those small particles of dust, and the lungs have no effective means of ejection.

You have heard of silicosis, of tuberculosis and pneumonia, of allergies, of catarrh, of asthma. Dust is a contributory cause of all those diseases. Dust carries germs with it right into those lungs of yours and your workers. Some of those germs are harmless and perform a useful function in nature. But many of them are harmful. Lister explained that dust is harmful chiefly because it carries harmful living germs. The really dangerous germs carried by dust are tuberculosis bacillus, streptococcus, pneumococcus, and diphtheria.

In some industrial plants the health laws require that the air be filtered. But such laws are not for offices, for the air in offices is not thought of as harmful. Yet it is harmful. It carries dust and dust-borne germs. And those germs send office workers home for the afternoon, for days and, yes, even for weeks.

3. Create desire

To you office managers those absences are a headache, a headache that plagues you particularly in the winter months. Yet you can cut down absenteeism by getting rid of the airborne dust in your offices. When employers understand what filtered air can do in keeping workers on the job, the office of the future will have air that is almost free of dust and dust-borne germs.

When an employee is absent, you lose two ways. Most of you pay her salary—there is a money loss. And then there is the loss of work. Further, there is the tremendous loss of efficiency in the half-hearted efforts of workers who are dragging with colds but do not go home.

Does filtered air cut down absenteeism due to colds and other respiratory diseases?
Well, the Ajax Industries with 222 employees in their offices filtered the air delivered to their offices and cut down absences by 46 per cent. The saving on time alone paid for the installation of the filtering equipment in the first six months. Mr. John Winns, who is here tonight, will confirm those figures. The Alyn Company, with over 100 employees in its offices, reports a reduction of lost time for colds of 42 per cent. Mr. Alyn himself—I believe he is an officer of your club—is a most enthusiastic booster of air filtering.

Is this filtering equipment expensive? No, it is not. For in every case it pays for itself in savings on lost time. Does its installation disturb office routine? No, it can be installed after working hours. Then why don't more companies use it?

Well, few people understand air filtering. When they do, they want it. And after they have had it for a while they ask, "Why didn't we do this long ago?"

4. Suggest action

Gentlemen, I could quote many figures and facts similar to those I gave you on the Ajax and Alyn Companies. But here is what I suggest. I have a list here of the companies that have filtered the air supplied to their office employees. I will give a copy of this to any one of you. Then I would suggest this. You ask the names on this list. Telephone them, or better still, make a personal call upon them. Check into what air filtering is doing for them. It might do the same for you.

Every one of you—if you have twenty or more office employees—can save money through air filtering. Here is my suggestion:

First: Look into it—check some companies that have tried it.
Second: If you think it might have possibilities for your company, put in a trial installation in one office.
Third: Keep records on absenteeism. Do those three things and without doubt you will show your company a big saving in money and in office efficiency.

(Note: This talk is written without benefit of the suggestions that come later in the book. But as this stands it would make a good talk.)

An electric-range salesman once told me that he followed the markings on his switches when he made a talk. He started with simmer, moved into low, dallied awhile in medium, then got into medium high, and wound up with a blaze on high. He had something there. The only question about his plan is that his simmer might not get the group on the edge of their chairs at the start. Most teachers of public speaking tell you that you have to knock them dead with the first sentence.

I can't say that I wholly agree with that. Surely, it is good to have a first sentence that slays them. It is better probably to have a first paragraph that gets them on the edges of their chairs. But I worry, too, about the balance of the speech. You have to hold interest all the way through the speech.

The electric-range salesman does have a big point. He builds up to the end. So often the speeches you hear are good at the start, but they seem to flicker out as they near the end. If you will study the formulas in this book you will find that all of them hold interest until the end. They start high by attracting attention and they build up until they ask for action.

Another useful formula is:

1. What happened in the past.
2. What happened today.
3. What will happen in the future.

This one is great for the extemporaneous speech. Let's say you are called upon to talk on a subject. You have nothing prepared. Well, worry not—start with the past, then talk about today, then about tomorrow. You can use that formula on almost any subject.

I have talked about enough formulas to give you the idea. First was the street hawker's:

1. Make them dissatisfied.
2. Suggest a remedy.
3. Answer questions and objections.
4. Ask for action.

The Negro preacher's went:

1. Tell them what you are going to tell them.
2. Tell them.
3. Tell them what you just told them.

The product-description formula went:

1. What it is.
2. What it does.
3. How to use it.

The AIDA formula went:

1. Attract attention.
2. Arouse interest.
3. Create desire.
4. Suggest action.

Then there is the one which will get you out of a hole if you are called upon without any notice at all.

1. What happened in the past.
2. What is happening today.
3. What will happen in the future.

Then the plan of the electric-range salesman:

1. Start on SIMMER.
2. Move into LOW.
3. Dally in MEDIUM.
4. Go into MEDIUM HIGH.
5. Finish in HIGH.

The other plan discussed was:

1. First things first.
2. Second things second.
3. Next things next.
4. Last things last.

Those seven formulas will give you a plan for almost any kind of speech you want to write. I have repeated them here so that you can look at them all at once and check on the one you want to use. Of course, these are not all the speech formulas in existence —not at all. Almost every book on speechmaking gives you one. Use any one you fancy, but my point is—use some formula. Give your speech a plan.

How do you use it? Well, you have laid out your speech on paper. Now decide on the formula you will use. Then arrange your material under the steps of the formula you selected. Here are some points to remember on this matter of plan.

1. A plan for your presentation makes for a better speech.
2. There are many formulas you can use for a speech.
3. The same formula will not apply to all kinds of speeches. You may need one formula for a speech that informs, another for a speech that entertains, a third for a speech that appeals for action.
4. A speech that starts toward its objective and keeps on the track is usually a good speech.

Now, let's get on to the next step. You know what material you have. You have selected the formula to use. But before you start writing, let's talk about slanting the speech to appeal to the audience's interest.

5. Their Interest, Not Yours

Everything you write in your speech should be written in terms of audience interest. What does that mean? Well, everything you say should be aimed at what the people out front are interested in. As I sit there listening to you make a speech, I'm interested in me. The fat fellow with the tight collar in the third row is interested in himself. His shoes hurt. He's tired. He's had too much lunch. The air is not too good, and he is logy, sleepy, ready to yawn. For that reason what you say must be more interesting to him than the two-minute nap that would make a new man out of him. You don't have a ghost of a show with that fellow if you talk about something that doesn't interest him. He sits there asking, "What does it mean to me?" or "What do I get out of it?" You will do better if you answer those questions.

How do you talk in terms of audience interest? Well, let's have a few examples. A mother says to her youngster, "I want you to wear your rubbers today."

"Why?" asks Junior.

"Because I don't want you down with a cold," the mother replies.

Junior thinks of the last time he had a cold. It wasn't so bad. He sat up in his bed all day. Every time he wanted anything, he called his mother and she climbed the stairs and brought him orange juice or grape juice or water and gave him ice cubes to suck. Then Uncle Looie brought him all those comic books. And Daddy came home with a lollypop, one of the big ones, every night. When Mother went to her bridge club, Mrs. Mittens came in and read him stories. No, it wasn't so bad at all.

Thus that answer of Mother's had little recognition of Junior's interest. But suppose Junior has been going to the movies every Saturday afternoon and is interested in the Dick Tracy serial. Last Saturday they left poor Dick hanging from a window ledge forty-four stories up, and Junior has talked about it all week and can hardly wait until the next episode to find out what has happened to his hero. Then when Junior asks why he should wear his rubbers, Mother says, "Well, if you get your feet wet and catch cold, you can't go to the movies on Saturday and find out what happened to Dick Tracy."

I don't think I need point out which of these two answers is more likely to get Junior to wear his rubbers.

It is easy for you to talk about your plan or idea in the way you yourself think of it. It is just as easy to slant those same thoughts to appeal to the audience.

There are a number of ways you can make sure you are talking in their interest. Here are some of the most common mistakes speakers make:

1. They speak of what they want, not what the audience wants.
2. They don't explain why it is to the audience's interest.
3. They don't use the right appeals.
4. They don't make the audience understand. Their points are made in terms that are not familiar to the audience.
5. They don't use the emotional appeal enough. There is too much of the factual and statistical.
6. They don't hit the group's interest soon enough.

Let's discuss the first point—they speak in terms of what they want, not what the audience wants. Now this is a simple thing, but it indicates how the speaker thinks about his subject. The speaker says, "I would like to tell you. . . ." He should say, "You will be interested to know. . . ." He goes on to state, "My opinion of this is. . . ." He should say, "You feel this way about it, don't you?" Get the idea? A man from the factory, presenting a product to a group of salesmen, is quite likely to say, "We give you this feature, and we have this. . . ." He should put it, "You have this feature to sell, and you have this. . . ." Not long ago I listened to a man make a presentation of his product. It was filled with "we's"—we did this—we gave you that—we advertised in this magazine—we have this display. When he asked me what I thought of the presentation, I suggested that he put it all in terms of the audience, that instead of those "we's" he use "you's." He looked at me and said, "Why didn't I think of that? It should be that way."

Now how would he do that? Well, here is a try at putting in the "you."

"You asked the factory for this and here it is—just what you asked for."

"You have this to sell."

"These advertisements in these magazines will be sending shoppers into your stores."

"Think how this display will look in your store."

That kind of talk would hold the interest of a salesman. It is slanted at his interest. When you talk about the display in his store, he starts to think of the corner in which he will put it. When you talk of the advertisement sending shoppers into the store, he thinks of the woman who came in with the advertisement in her hand and wanted to see the appliance. When you talk in his interest he goes along with you. Why, then, show that you are thinking of yourself first by saying, "I would like to tell you . . ."? Say instead, "Here is news. Maybe you have heard it and maybe not, but, boy, it is important to you."

It is not quite enough to change the wording from "we" to "you." We had better make sure that with the change in wording we explain why. Let's say that you are making a speech about a plan that will build up your club. To put the plan in effect you need a change in the by-laws or an increase in dues. That is a project that needs some selling. I belong to this club. I am satisfied with things as they are. I don't see any sense in changing the by-laws. And I am not ever in favor of paying more dues. Well, if you want to change me over, you had better tell me what it means to me, and you had better do the best job of explaining you know how to do.

How will I gain? In money, in savings, in esteem of my fellow townsmen, in satisfaction because I am a part of a worthy project, in comfort, in better meetings, better food at the dinners, better speakers, in prestige, in knowledge, in joy in a job well done.

Those are some of the appeals you had better use and explain when you ask me to vote for the change in the by-laws and the increase in dues. But don't tell me that I will get a lot of joy and satisfaction out of these changes. Explain the joy and describe it specifically, explain the satisfaction and describe it in detail. In the electrical-appliance business, salesmen use the word "economical" a lot. Usually the word needs explanation. They say that an electric-range oven is economical. They mean that it uses electricity only nine minutes out of the hour, or that all the heat is used, that all of it goes into the pan, or that none of it goes up the flue. In such explanations "economical" is not enough. The statement needs explanation. And that is what I mean by explanation in this speech.

In the speech to influence the audience to do something, you have to tell them why it is to their interest and then explain so that they understand. They won't accept your statement. They want proof. Yes, explain how this plan will build the club, how it will make good publicity for them, how it will bring the club to the top in community activities, how it may build up one of the members so that he can run for Senator. But don't stop with saying that it will—explain *how* it will. Such explanations will hold their interest. Tell them what it means to them, then *explain* what it means to them, and you will hold interest from beginning to end.

That's what you must do in any talk. You can't talk in generalities and hold interest, no matter how loud you shout. Speak not of hunger in China or the faraway places. Start hunger gnawing at the innards of the bald man in the second row. Don't rave about athlete's foot in general. Start his feet itching. When you do that you have his interest. Think of the street peddler selling the exerciser and take a lesson from him. Make the audience feel with you.

Remember that many speakers fail to slant their talk at the interest of the audience. The young man studying selling is taught that there are a number of reasons why people buy. These might be listed as:

To save time
To save labor
To satisfy appetites
To increase respect of others
To improve appearance
To be considered good sports
To save what they have

If your subject has any appeal for any one of these reasons, write in that appeal. Here is what I mean.

Let's take the last one, "To save what they have." You are healthy; you want to maintain your health. I do, everybody does, and so health is a sure-fire interest arouser. But the health of the public as a whole will not have too much interest. It's my health that I am interested in. Talk my health in good, common-sense, everyday language and I will listen with interest to what you say.

Talks on technical subjects like health must be put in terms that can be understood. Here's an example. For years, health authorities had been talking about vitamin content of vegetables. They had been giving nutrition courses in which they taught the various vitamin classifications. You saw long tables of what vegetables had this vitamin and what vegetables had that vitamin. Homemakers took these courses; they passed examinations. They knew vitamins, but very few of the students knew what to do about them.

There was nothing wrong with these courses. The teaching methods were good. The appeal was there—health. Every student wanted to keep his health or improve it. But the idea was not explained in everyday terms that the homemakers understood. Then some wise person started teaching vitamin content in terms of cooking. Every homemaker knew how to cook. When it was explained that the vitamins in vegetables were good for her family, she was interested. When it was further explained that when she bought the vegetables in the store they were rich in vitamin content but that most of that content was lost in her method of preparation of the vegetables in her kitchen, she wanted to know what

she did that was wrong. Now the teachers could explain that vitamin content of vegetables was injured by too much water or too
much heat or too much air and she understood. When she was told
to use little or no water, to bring to a boil quickly, and then cook on
low heat, to cook in covered utensils and not to stir, she understood.
When the vitamin story was brought into her kitchen and she was
shown how to cook certain vegetables so that the vitamin content
was retained, the homemaker had a much better chance of understanding. She might not get interested in Vitamin A, or niacin or
thiamin or riboflavin—those were strange names—but if too much
water, or too much boiling, or stirring, or cooking in open utensils
without lids would lose that vitamin content she could do something about it.

Through such an approach the vitamin story was explained to
the American homemaker in wartime. It was the same speakers,
the same voices, in the same lecture rooms, but what a difference.
Explained technically, the vitamin story seemed unreal. By tying
it into the daily lives of homemakers and their most important job
—cooking the meals for their families—the story had interest and
was understood.

Each member of an audience sits out there asking, "What does
it mean to me?" or "What do I get out of it?" And so as you
talk you have to answer those questions. It is not too difficult to
do that, for there are many motives that you can appeal to. Some
of them are emotional, some based on good common sense. But you
must select some of those motives and use them when you make
your appeal. A list of motives and a description of how you can
appeal to each would take a whole book. Here is a list of motivating forces that you might bring into play: affection, duty,
gain, fear, pride, selfishness, appetite, respect of others, appearance, security, saving. With such a list it will not be difficult to
take any material you have and slant your appeal so that it hits
the audience in terms of its interest.

For example, you are talking on oil heat, on its benefits and
advantages. As you look over the list above you see that you can
appeal to affection—oil heat would be good for the loved ones.

Perhaps you can work up an argument on duty. Gain would be simple if you could show a decrease in costs and a greater convenience. Pride—ah yes, the purchaser would be happy to show his purchase to the neighbors. Selfishness—perhaps not in so many words, but there is personal comfort, and leisure, and ease of use. Respect of others—you bet, keeping up with the Joneses. Appearance—it improves the property, gives it a greater productive value. There is an economy of use, a saving of time, of labor.

I don't know much about oil heat. I purposely selected a subject I did not know too well. But as you look over that list you see how easy it is to slant this subject at the interests of the audience. Why not take the subject you have selected for your next speech and go through that list of motives? You will find that there are many ways you can change your treatment of the subject matter to make it answer the questions of the audience, "What does it mean to me?" and "What do I get out of it?"

In training, salesmen are taught that there are certain buying motives. They are asked to describe a product feature. Then they are asked, "What does that mean to a shopper?" Now they reshape the description so that it has shopper appeal. That's what you have to do with your speech material. Take a statement that you have worked up to use in the talk and ask yourself the question, "What does it mean to this Joe in the audience?" Then shape it to appeal to him.

At about this point you may say, "Look here, you are talking about salesmen all the time. I'm not a salesman." I grant that. But most of the talks you have to make are to persuade somebody to do something. To vote, to change the by-laws, to raise the dues, to come to the golf picnic—you are asking them to do something. And those requests are selling jobs. You have to sell them on what you want them to do. So bear with me while I give these selling examples. It will do you good to learn something about selling.

Of the list of appeals to action, the emotional ones should not be overlooked. It is fine to marshal all the facts and statistics and to prove the logic of your case. But remember that a lot of things are bought on emotional reasoning. Here is a partial list of such appeals.

MATERIAL GAIN: You probably would mention this one first.

ROMANCE: Two bottles and you'll be a beauty. The toupee that nobody will notice. The success course that will have the boys rushing you.

HEALTH: The bounding energy. You never feel tired. You hit the golf ball two miles, and straight.

EMULATION: You are the one the others copy. You they admire. They ask your opinion. They take your orders.

SAFETY: You protect your health. You protect your life. You save little old you.

COMFORT: You sit on your front porch in the easy chair. All you do is press a button—and perhaps you can get somebody to do that for you.

SENSORY PLEASURE: It tastes good. It feels grand. It looks swell. It sounds beautiful. It smells too.

CURIOSITY: Did you know this? The $64 question.

DOMESTIC HAPPINESS: The wife and kids. The chance to do something for them, to show you love them.

Don't neglect these appeals when you are writing your speech. Some of them might help. Remember the brothers who want to be the life of the party, who want to be free of halitosis or dandruff, who want the wife and kids to think they are grand. Those desires are natural. Perhaps your logic and statistics will slay them, but add a dash of emotional appeal too. A man may claim that he doesn't want his name or photograph in the newspaper, but just listen to him when the friends around the club start to kid him about the piece or the photograph.

The emotional appeal is good and so are any others that help you put your talk in terms of the interest of the audience. It is well to establish that interest quickly.

Let's say you plan to talk on job security. You have gathered a wealth of statistics. You have the facts to wow your audience. Let's say you start like this:

> Gentlemen: Last year, in this town with a population of 10,000 employables, 25 per cent of that number changed jobs. Two per cent of that number changed of their own volition. But get this—the remaining 23 per cent were laid off, furloughed, or discharged without having one word to say about it.

That is startling, isn't it? Your information is good and it should have some appeal, for every man in the room has a job. But stated in this way, the audience will not get too wildly excited about it, so let's try again.

> Gentlemen, how secure is that job of yours? Are you on the same job you held one year ago? Well, if you are you are lucky, for one out of every four workers in this town has changed in the past year. And almost every one of them had nothing to say about the change. They were fired, discharged, furloughed, or laid off. They didn't want to change. But they had to.

That's a little better, isn't it? But let's see if we can't sock them a little harder and sit them on the edge of their chairs. Here goes.

> Today I lost my job. Tomorrow you may lose yours.
> Now what would you do if you had to go home tomorrow night and tell the little woman and the kids, "I got laid off today." Perhaps the boss said furloughed. But how would you feel? Low, wouldn't you?
> Yet that's exactly what happened to one out of every four workers in this town last year. One out of four—fired, discharged, furloughed, laid off. Those men didn't want to change any more than you do as you sit here tonight. But they did change.

That's enough to give you the idea. Get the talk started quickly in terms of their interest. Lose no time in telling them that it is to their interest to listen. Get their interest with the first paragraph, and hit them hard.

Now let's go over the points in this chapter again.

1. Remember that the audience sits there asking, "What does it mean to me?"
2. Don't speak of "we" or "I"—use "you." What you want is of no interest to them. It is what they want that interests them.
3. Tell why it is to their interest, and *explain* why it is to their interest. Make them understand.
4. Search for the big appeals—the factual ones and the emotional ones.
5. Translate the appeal in terms that the audience will understand. Don't talk Greek to them unless they are Greeks.
6. Use the emotional appeals. They are powerful, motivating forces.
7. In your first sentence get over the idea that the group is interested in your subject. Don't start with a lot of preliminary blah-blah. Get their interest early.

With interest of the audience in mind, suppose you go back over that outline you laid out on paper and make notes in each of your squares, telling you why each point appeals to this audience. Let the note remind you how you are going to cover the point so that you answer their question, "What does it mean to me?"

Now that we have our material laid out, have selected a formula for the presentation, and have studied our material to find its greatest appeal to the audience, let's discuss the kind of writing we have to do.

6. Write It to Joe

At the start let's write this speech to Joe. We'll pick out a typical Joe from your audience, a fellow who is a fairly good composite of the group. Then we'll write our speech directly to Joe.

How do you think of the group to whom you're going to talk? Perhaps you think of them as gentlemen and scholars. Again as brothers. Or maybe more familiarly as "you guys" or "you lugs." But no matter how you have them pegged, there is one Joe among them who is a cross section of all of them.

Let's put the words down on paper just as you would speak them to Joe. Write the word "Joe" up there at the start of the first paragraph, put a comma behind it, and write:

> Joe, as I stand up here on the platform tonight I can think of the time a few years ago when I met you in Kansas City. Remember, Joe? It was in that little restaurant with the blonde waitress. I still remember, Joe, what you said that night.

Would Joe and a group of Joes listen to a story like that? You know they would. And whenever you start off so closely to this Joe's thoughts and interests, you are certain to get attention. Once I heard a speaker start a talk to a group of his dealers with, "Gentlemen and Chiselers." He smiled when he said it, of course, but the crowd roared. He was talking right down their alley. And all through the talk you could see that this man had thought of the Joes out in front of him when he was writing it to the one Joe who was a composite of the group. He wrote it just as he would talk to that Joe face to face. His talk was on the beam every minute.

Writing to Joe, you keep your talk on a conversational level. Sit him across the desk and talk to him as you write. You can't go high-hat on a guy across the desk. You won't get up in the blue sky, over his head, if you imagine he is right there talking to you, asking a question now and then. Putting in an argument occasionally. Adding a thought or two. No, you'll keep down to earth where your talk belongs.

This goes for any kind of audience. All groups are made up of Joes. You may be talking to bankers, lawyers, merchant chiefs, rich men, poor men, beggarmen, or thieves. But in each group there is an average Joe. Pick out that individual and write your speech to him.

If you feel that you have to talk big language to big shots, you're all wrong. For big shots talk about the cost of turkey, about the mashie shot they missed last Sunday, about how tough it is to get good liquor. Listen to a group of these fellows talk and you'll find they don't talk much differently than you and your buddies do. So if you will just write to this Joe, you'll get your story over to the entire audience.

How do you do that? Well, here's an example:

> Joe, as you picked up your newspaper this morning I'll bet this thought crossed your mind. . . .

That gets you off to a start. You're talking to him about his newspaper. And his name helps you keep right on the beam.

Put Joe's name in every sentence in this talk of yours and you won't get off on a side track. How to do that? Well, look:

> No, Joe, such a grievance cries aloud for vengeance. But, Joe, you can't do anything rash. No, Joe, you've got to play safe, to hold back. And that holding back gives you an opportunity, Joe, to show how big you are.

There it is with "Joe" in every sentence. Now let's see what we have with the "Joes" out.

> No, such a grievance cries aloud for vengeance. But you can't do anything rash. No, you've got to play safe, to hold back. And that holding back gives you an opportunity to show how big you are.

It's still on the beam. It's still talking to Joe just as much as was the other. But putting Joe's name in there has helped you keep on the beam.

When you're writing Joe in, you're talking directly to him. You're not so likely to bring in those big words of which you are not too sure. You're not so likely to use quotations which you yourself feel are the bunk. You're not so likely to tell a funny story which you know for sure doesn't advance your point.

So let's write it to Joe. You may want to talk turkey to him. You may want to get tough. You many want to praise him, to cajole, or persuade him. And you can do any one of those jobs better if you write him in.

So what we're talking about here is not just trying to keep Joe in mind. It's to write him down on paper.

"Now listen, Joe—."

"And, Joe, where does that get you?"

"Look, Joe, here's the way you do it."

"Let's discuss this thing, Joe."

That's the way you do it. It's an easy way to write. Just like a letter home. It's conversational, it's brass tacks. Write Joe into every sentence, every thought. It will give life to your speech. It will keep you close to earth. Write it to Joe and your talk will come much closer to ringing the bell.

7. Use Your Own Words

There are a lot of reasons why you should use your own language in a speech. Here are a few:

You will sound natural.
Your own words are more likely to convey your meaning.
You will impress the group with your sincerity.
You can pronounce your own words.

Not long ago one of the boys was giving a talk before a group of fellows in the office. Somewhere in that speech he had written a sentence which started, "This epitomizes. . . ." It came like a bolt out of the blue. The audience started in shocked surprise. This was not Pete, their pal, their friend. This was some stuffed shirt who looked like Pete, sounding off with big words. They didn't titter at Pete's big words or smile politely. No, the brothers laughed out loud.

Many times, in conversation with my youngsters, I have used words not normally used in conversation with them. The kids, much like these friends of Pete's, never fail to rush forth with the razzberry. Of course, when you deliver your speech, your audience will not do that for you. They'll let you go on, give you rope, and shrug their shoulders. Because it's your speech. But you can't assume you're fooling them because they don't let you know. No, they spot you, peg you for the phony you are, and rate your cause along with you.

Your own words are more likely to convey your meaning. The other day a newspaper reporter interviewed a friend of mine. The friend gave him a statement. Later, when the reporter wrote it from the notes, he asked me, "What's this fellow trying to cover up?" I checked with the man who gave the statement and found that he wasn't trying to cover up anything. The chance to talk to a reporter was too much for him and he talked in big words, which, when tied together end-to-end, meant nothing. If he hadn't been swept off his feet by the fact that he was giving an interview, he might have used his own words and told the reporter exactly what he meant. But asked to furnish information, he set out to make an impression and what he said in his Sunday vocabulary added up to zero.

Perhaps in some speeches you will want to tell the audience nothing. But that's not the kind of speech we are discussing. When you want to cover up, dust off the glittering generalities and put them to work. But don't go highbrow when you are writing a speech to tell Joe Doakes how to sell his product or to get Joe steamed up about contributing to the Community Fund. Remember always that when you use your own words, you can come closer to saying exactly what you mean.

Another advantage in using your own words is that you can pronounce them. I once used the word "nutritious" in the script of a speech written for another man. In rehearsal we discovered that the man who was to use the speech couldn't say "nutritious." Every time he came to it he stumbled. We tried it again and again and then changed to "more healthful." The meaning wasn't exactly the same, but he could pronounce the words. If you use your own words, you won't be stuck with a word you can't pronounce.

I have trouble with the word "statistics." Somehow it seems to get tangled with my tongue. A speaker friend, with the ability to make audiences love him, has a list of words that he claims get tangled with his upper plate. He has placed taboos on all of them. If professional speakers will go to this trouble, the amateur should at least hesitate before he writes a word like "gregarious" into his script.

Your own words sound sincere. Remember that when you give this talk you have to mean what you say. If you say, "The world is made of green cheese," you have to say it as if you mean it. It has to sound to the people in your audience as if you mean it. Now the best way to make such a statement sound right is to use your own words.

In working on juries, I have noticed how police, in testifying, always use the word "observe." You no doubt have met personally the tough traffic officer who can ask in such an expressive tone, "Where's the fire?" On the stand the same man will say, "I was standing on the corner when I observed this car—."

Probably under any other condition the cop would say, "I saw this man." He'd sound much more natural if he did. Perhaps the word "observe" carries a more exact meaning, or it may be legally correct for the record. But it is not a word you would expect from a cop. The same may be true of many of the exact words you would use for a common word—your substitution may give your meaning more exactly, but it doesn't sound right to the audience and it makes you sound stiff and unnatural.

One way to see how the words sound is to dictate the speech to a wire or tape recorder. Then play back the speech. One of my friends did this with a series of radio commercials he had written and which he had to read. He played each of them, studying them as the tape talked back to him. When he had listened to all of them he said, "I knew the meaning of all the words, but they did not sound sincere."

Sincerity is a big asset in a talk. If you are pleading for a cause you must sound as if you believe. You can't be a man on his feet, mouthing hollow words. Just try to say the following passage. Read it aloud. Try to put some sincerity into it.

> In his panoramic and generalizing qualities, he is a true son of the age of the grandiose and the monumental in art, memorializing the triumph of the enlightment and of the humanist and liberal tradition.

Those are not my words. They are selected from a piece in a weekly magazine. I am not sure what they mean. To me they seem to call for the comment of the sharecropper housewife to the magazine-subscription solicitor who had just read a list of the names of the editorial staff: "Read 'em again, son, they sure sound pretty."

You need that ring of sincerity in what you say. Your speech must sound as if you believe. That's true whether you are talking cause, product, advertising, anything—for or against. If it does not sound as if you believe, why should the audience believe? And no matter how much you practiced, you could not make that passage above sound as if you meant it. Yet at your service club next week or next month you will hear a speaker who is using words that are not his, words just as meaningless when he says them as the ones quoted above.

Perhaps you have taken part in a conference where a club, an organization, or a company is trying to fashion a statement of policy which one of the group is to use in a speech. If you have, you know what I mean. Joe writes the original statement. Then the group meets and he reads it. Each sits wisely listening. Now one makes a note, then another. When Joe finishes, he asks for comments. Andy starts. He says, "Joe, it's a swell statement, but. . . ." Andy lists his comments. Abe, Bill, and Charlie follow suit. They all start, "It's swell, but. . . ." When they finish, Joe wonders what was swell about it. For the statement is in shreds and if it is rewritten it is not one half so good as it was when Joe started reading.

Always when I am in one of these round-and-rounds, I chuckle inwardly. For Joe is going to make the speech anyway. He is going to follow some of the suggestions, but not all of them. If he followed all of them he might just as well stand up and recite, "Baa, baa, black sheep. . . ." For the revision is certainly not in his words. And if Joe is going to make the speech and he is going to make it sound right, he must do it in his own words.

That's why it is so difficult to write a speech jointly. You know the story about the two executives who brought the letter to the boss to be approved. It was to go out to all the customers, but they wanted him to see it before it was sent down to be printed.

The boss read the letter slowly. Then he asked, "Who wrote this?"

"We did—jointly," one of the executives replied.

"That's what I thought," the boss commented. "And the joint comes right about in the middle of this paragraph."

That's the argument for getting all the speech, every word of it, in your language. You don't want the audience to hear the joints creak.

I make a number of speeches around the country and I find that there are a lot of the other fellow's words in the introductions I get. In many cases they have the club wit introduce me. He goes to town on how difficult I am to get as a speaker. Since I have to earn a living on a job that does not include speaking before organizations such as his, there is truth as well as humor in what he says. These humorous introductions never seem to get off the track. It is the serious ones that stray afield. I suppose it is because the man who is assigned the job has but a few words to organize. And so he does his paragraph and then polishes and polishes it until it shines.

Not long ago one of my friends in introducing me to an audience said, "This man is one of the leaders in the field known as sales training." Then after a few words on what sales training is, and the need for it, he went on, "Mastery of this exhaustive subject is not to be easily attained."

I said this man was a friend of mine. He was not trying to sabotage. Yet that is what he came out with. If he had been introducing me to a friend he would have said, "This is Ed Hegarty. He is a sales training expert. He's an expert among experts." But my friend had written his introduction. He had dug up some high-sounding words for the occasion. It didn't sound like him—he's a regular Joe. And it didn't give the audience the picture of me he wanted them to have. Always use your own words—even when you have but a short blurb to do. They won't throw you. And they won't stamp you as a stuffed shirt.

Many times I have been asked to rehearse talks that were to be part of a meeting. I always welcome such rehearsals because it provides a chance to go through the talk once and to get outside comment. At times those comments suggest word changes. One time I remember I said, "This is important. . . ." The critic suggested that I say, "This is of prime importance. . . ."

I said, "Look, I never use the word 'prime,' but if you feel that some accent is needed I will try to find another way of saying that."

I could have said "of real importance" or "it's most important," but "prime" was not one of my words. Certainly I know what "prime" means and perhaps I could have used the word, but I would never have felt right doing so. We settled by making the statement, "This is the most important point in the whole procedure." I could say that without thinking that it was not exactly right for me. That's when you stumble—when you are thinking about what you are saying. If you have to make a statement just so, with exact wording, with emphasis on certain points, the audience will sense it.

But they won't razz you if you get off the beam. As a rule, the audience is courteous. A salesman friend of mine had been calling on a certain company for a long time. He had been trying to get in to see the boss, but always an assistant took him in hand and kept him out of the big man's office. Then one day as he walked through a trade show he saw the big man. He went over to him, introduced himself, and stated that he'd called on the company a number of times.

"Do they treat you courteously?" asked the boss.

"That they do," the salesman replied. "They kill me with courtesy, but they don't give me any business."

And that's the thing you have to keep in mind as you make your speech. The audience will be courteous. No matter what kind of language you use, they'll sit quietly and appear to listen, perhaps with interest. But they won't buy your deal. So if you want to get them to do something, if you want them to carry a message home, to get enthused about your cause, you had better explain it in your own words. Perhaps in an anecdote you plan to say that a man was soused, plastered, spifficated, or stewed to the gills. Okay, there's no complaint on that if those are your words. But don't write any of those words with quotes around them.

Why? I don't want you to have any words in your talk which you think of as foreign to your vocabulary. If it is your practice to say that a man is intoxicated or inebriated, write it that way; but if you can say that the man was stewed to the gills without slipping out of character, write it so without quotes.

The other day I was asked to go over the script of a talk. At the end of the first page I came across the expression "Confidentially, it stinks." The expression was in quotes.

"Why the quotes?" I asked.

The writer wasn't sure.

"How would you say it in your own words?" I continued.

He thought awhile, "Well, I'd say it just that way."

I asked him to say, "Confidentially, it stinks." He did it easily and naturally.

"You say it naturally," I went on. "Then why do you put quotes around it when you write it?"

Now I wasn't arguing with him about the quotes in his talk. I have no battle with quotes when they belong. But I was quite certain that if he thought about those words in quotes, he wouldn't use them as if they were his. He would speak them as if they were foreign to him, and he would lose the punch the words would give.

Many times you have heard speakers say, "In the vernacular . . ." or, "As the boys on Tenth Avenue would say. . . ." Such qualifications are excess baggage. If the boys on Tenth Avenue would say it, perhaps the boys on Park, or Fifth or Sixth or Seventh would say it too. By such expressions the speaker advertises that he is in the wrong ball park.

Usually when you write quotes around a word you do it not because the word belongs in quotes, but because you are thinking of the word as one that should be in quotes, because it is not quite the thing for a speech. If you think of any word or any expression that doesn't belong, leave it out of your talk. If, in private conversation, you'd say, "The guy is nuts," and you want to use the expression to describe him in your speech, don't think of it with quotes setting it apart. If it's natural for you to use 'these expressions, write them in. But if you never make a crack like that in private conversation, put quotes around it. Then the quotes belong.

One way to stick to your own words is to use a dictating machine or to dictate the script to your secretary. In this way you talk your speech. If you keep on talking without stopping to think of the exact meaning of words or to think of what you are saying, you should come up with a script that is in your own words.

The best words are short words, words with positive meaning. Words of one syllable are good because they are your words, my words, everybody's words. In a talk I do on "The Language of Selling," I have a routine I do on small words. With it I use a chart which illustrates how we live in small words. This chart reads:

```
Ring—wake—live—day—light
wake—look—see—shave—bath
primp—dress—eat—walk—ride
work—sale—ring—pay—play
sing—laugh—cry—love—hate
bed—sleep—snore—dream.
```

I use the chart to describe the day of the average salesman in words of one syllable. You can say almost anything in words of that kind. And many times two or three of the small words will do the job of the fancy word and do it better. You always have a better chance to be understood with the small word.

It is not too difficult to dig words out of books and put them together in a way that sounds beautiful as you hear them—beautiful to you, anyway. Not long ago one of my friends used the expression "correlate together" in a talk. He fancied that word "correlate" and he had written it into his speech. But when he used it, he proved to his audience that it wasn't his and that he did not know what it meant.

Let's review these suggestions again.

1. Use your own words; don't look up any in the dictionary.
2. Don't try to use large words; the small words are best. You understand them and so does the audience.

3. Use words that you can pronounce. Remember your thick tongue or your upper plate.
4. Try for the ring of sincerity. Your own words will give that to you.
5. Try recording the speech on a wire, tape, or record recorder.
6. Don't try to write a speech with another. The joints will show.
7. When you have to introduce a speaker at your service club, don't write a lot of eyewash about him. Do it in your own words—simply.
8. Use slang if it is natural to you. Don't use such expressions as "As the boys on Tenth Avenue would say." Usually those fellows express themselves in an understandable way.
9. Don't think of any word or phrase you use as being in quotes unless the quotes are there for emphasis.
10. Use the simplest words you know. Words of one syllable are wonderful.

At the start we promised to make this speech-writing job easy. Right now we rule out looking for words—you will use your own vocabulary—your words, not mine. That will be one of your short cuts in getting this speech down on paper.

8. Spoken, Not Written, Language

You have to speak this speech, so as we start let's try to lay off written words. We want spoken words—words that you would normally use in speech, words that others would normally use in speech. This may illustrate what I mean. In my speech on "How to Run a Sales Meeting" I do a sequence on this point. I ask the audience how many can tell me what the word "fatuous" means. I ask those who can to raise their hands. When I ask that question the faces of the audience are blank. I ask them to raise their hands. Then I repeat the word and spell it out. This time I do get a ripple of recognition. Next I hold up a card on which the word is spelled out. Now, because they see the word spelled out, more of them know the word I mean. I use the stunt to show the difference between spoken and written words. "Fatuous" means silly. Fatuous is a written word—a word your audience might understand if they saw it written out. Silly is a word your audience will understand when you speak it.

One night after I had finished the speech in which I did this demonstration, a young lady came up to me and said, "It's certainly fatuous to use a silly word like fatuous when you want to say something is silly."

While I have taken a word here that is a bit unusual, the same principle applies to many simple words. When writing a speech, don't write, "The expenditures are X dollars annually." Put it, "The expenditures are X dollars every year." The audience will hear the two words better than the one and they will be more likely to understand what you mean. You may slur over the annually, or say it too fast. The same applies to "daily"; write "every day." For "necessarily" write "are necessary" or "are needed."

Since the writing of most of us is confined to business letters, probably the best way to illustrate the difference between written and spoken language is to recall the business letters we write. You'd never think of telephoning Joe Whosis and saying, "Joe, I have yours of recent date" or "Yours of the first instant is now in front of me." Perhaps you don't write letters like that. But here is a gem I took from a sales letter that reached me the other day: "This course is the result of the collective effort of outstanding executives. It will undoubtedly react to the financial advantage of those who avail themselves of the opportunity afforded." Now that is letter-writing language, but it won't do for a speech. Just stop now and try to say those words. The man speaking those two sentences to an audience would sound like a stuffed shirt.

That's the trouble with most of us when we sit down to write. We are stuffy. We grope for words. We don't open up. Let's take that paragraph from a letter and write it so that it would go over well in a speech. All he says is that some executives wrote the course, and that the man who gets the letter can cash in on the time and money he puts in to take it. Okay, let's write it thus— "This course was written by experts. If you pay the five-dollar enrollment fee and attend the six sessions, you will learn something that will help you earn more money."

That is a fast revision that no doubt can be bettered, but as the two sentences are now written they can be spoken more easily and can be quickly understood. If the main writing you do is in the business letters you dictate, this illustration gives you a suggestion as to why you must snap out of your usual writing routine.

The tendency to use written words is demonstrated almost every time one of our generals, admirals, or big business leaders gets a spot on the radio. We hear such mouthings as, "Let that traditional friendship be cemented and strengthened and buttressed by mutual labors in behalf of world peace." Out of one five-minute spot last night I picked these gems—"dawn of a new era"—"despondent and discordant world"—"relax no effort." I'm certain that most of our generals, admirals, and tycoons don't talk that way to their friends. How many times have you smiled at some of the words assigned to such casual performers on the radio as the truck driver testifying for the cough remedy? That's what you are flirting with when you use your writing vocabulary in a speech. Listen to Lowell Thomas tonight. I'm sure he knows all the big words, but note the ones he uses.

Another demonstration of the difficulty of speaking certain words so that they will be understood comes from the radio commercial. Look at the trouble they have with products with difficult-to-pronounce names. He spells it once, he spells it twice, and spells it once again. In television he holds up a card so that you can read it for yourself.

I have always held the theory that the announcer should write his own commercials. Then the words would be spoken words—his spoken words. He could eliminate the adjectives, he would discard the dangling phrases, he would use only words that he knew he could hang on to. At times you hear the dear wife growl at a commercial. Next time she does that try to analyze what the announcer said. Nine times out of ten you will find that it is the wording. The man isn't talking like a man. He sounds as if his mouth were full of mush—written-word mush. Yes, he is trying to speak written words.

Once we were recording a highly technical script for a sound film. There were thirty minutes of it, and when the narrator had it all on the record he threw the script on the floor and cried, "That's the first time I ever talked Greek for thirty minutes." I imagine that a lot of announcers feel like that about some of the material they have to read.

If you write for a living you will probably have a tougher time writing your speech in spoken words. For, brother, you have a vocabulary and you can't make too much use of a vocabulary in a speech that is going to be popular with your audience. Most writers are afflicted with a whole family of odd words. "Fatuous" may be one of them, but there are such words as "ordure," "insouciance," "truncate," "nuance." Don't think I picked those out of a dictionary, though I'll confess that I had to go to the dictionary to check on the spelling and find out what two of them meant.

Those words came out of speeches. I wrote them down as the men said them. They are not speech words. When you write them and I can see them in type, I have a chance to study them as well as hear them. But when you speak them at me, you overwhelm me.

If you are an advertisement writer, you'll have to hold back with all you have. You can't say "trouble-free service." You can't use those gems of fine writing like "There's eager yet thrilling power in the advanced V-8 cylinder engine" or "The gleaming white porcelain actually laughs off dirt and stain." Those phrases may be fine for the printed page, but they don't belong in the spoken speech. Similarly you might write, "He was a mousy, timorous sort of guy." In print that sentence is description. But if you are writing it to speak, better write it, "He was a mouse, and not a very brave mouse at that." If you would describe the man as mature, better change it to "old," "middle aged," or "about thirty-five."

Another point to consider is that the audience must hear and understand the word in the time it takes you to say it. They can't stop and study it, for you are on to other words and other thoughts. Thus any word you use must be one that can be understood in the time it takes you to say it. Use a familiar spoken word and they get it quickly; use an unfamiliar written word and they may not understand at all.

I can illustrate this point with two words which indicate size —"big" and "small." There are a lot of words that can be used to give the same thought, perhaps not exactly, but still close. Here are a number that could be used for "small":

diminutive	petty	squat
microscopic	elfin	minute
tiny	spare	embryonic
wee	stunted	little

Any one of that list might be a good written word. But only a few of them will qualify as spoken words. "Small" is good, and "little" is good, "tiny" might do, perhaps "wee," but any of the others might get lost when you speak them.

Now for a number of words that could be used for "large":

huge	colossal	capacious
enormous	great	spacious
big	bulky	corpulent
giant	voluminous	immense
Brobdingnagian	ample	vast
gargantuan	massive	tremendous

There are a few more possibles in that list. "Large" and "big" and "great." Right here you may say, "Wait a minute, Hegarty, you are going too far." Perhaps I am. But in many speeches I hear the words "ample" and "vast." As yet I have not heard a place where they belong. "Immense" will talk well and so will "enormous." "Tremendous" will also. But I would advise you to stop there.

Now I don't ask you to take my word for this. Listen to the speakers you hear. Note how many of them use words like "huge" and "vast." Note also how much better "large" or "big" would have been in the same place.

Written language has many ways of slipping into speeches. In telling stories you hear a speaker use such expressions as "he remarked" or "he retorted" or "he replied." In speaking it would be better to use "said" each time. "She said" and "I said" and then some more of the same. In writing, the variations of "said" cut down the repetition. But in speaking, those same variations sound formal or stilted and take away from the life of the story.

Perhaps you want to take a few stories out of the joke book, that speaker's friend you bought when you thought that someday you might have to make a speech. That's fine—that's where other speakers get those same stories. But if you lift that story, try to learn to tell it in spoken words, not in the words you find in the book.

As an advertising writer you'll have trouble with adjectives. You can't throw an adjective in front of a noun and feel that you have taken care of the problem. You may have to use another sentence or two to complete your thought. "Crystal-clear, flint-like hard-

ness" or "exactly right, well-groomed look" or "healthful, invigor-
ating tingle" may be okay for your printed piece, but as speech
material such descriptions are not. Even persons who write for a
living don't talk like that.

Here is a sentence of the kind I mean. It is part of a description
of a fine refrigerator:

"The blue-on-chrome nameplate blends with the blue-and-
chrome trim of the spacious interior."

As a written sentence that might get by. But if you were to use
it as a part of a speech it would be better thus:

"Look at that nameplate—blue on chrome. And look how it
matches the inside of the refrigerator. The inside is blue and chrome
too. And look at the room in that food compartment."

There are more words, yes. But you will have to use more words
in spoken language. The writer has the advantage over the speaker.
The writer can say it all by using a few adjectives. But the speaker
trying to use those adjectives will find himself in trouble. He will
either emphasize the adjective or emphasize the noun and the
partner that was to carry some of the load will be lost.

In the written piece you will find such expressions as "It is not
only this, it is also that." In spoken language the "not only" should
be cut out. It is far better to say, "It is this. And it is also that."
The audience may hear that "not" and then little more of the
sentence.

The same applies to the negative words like "unhappy." It is
better speech material to write it, "She is not happy." Instead of
"unsuccessful" use "not successful" or "without success." The
audience may not get the first syllable. It is always better to "accentuate the positive."

Just a short time ago I heard two fellows commenting on a
speaker. One said, "He can't talk for sour apples." The other said,
"Yeah, but he uses such beautiful phrases." Now those two men
were not speech coaches or literary critics, just two members of
the audience that had listened to a speaker.

Don't worry too much about the exact meaning of words. Perhaps it is stronger to say that a man "affirms" rather than "says," but

the audience will understand the latter. Many men pride themselves on the use of words that express the speaker's exact meaning. In a speech those exact meanings may be lost entirely.

Those dangling phrases that you find in writing have no place in a speech. You know the kind: "The knobs are knurled, assuring even pressure over the whole surface"—or "The shelves are adjustable, assuring flexibility for changing storage needs." Those are not spoken words. The man who says them is talking like a circular or an advertisement. So let's not write them in.

And while we are discussing the dangling phrases, introductory phrases like the first part of this sentence are not good speech material either. As speech material the preceding sentence would be best written:

"Introductory phrases are not good speech material. They are just as bad as dangling phrases."

Here are some more examples.

"With the marked trend in design toward massiveness that looks like more for the money, Westinghouse is in step with its new line of electric ranges."

As speech material it would be stronger thus:

"The new Westinghouse ranges look larger. They are larger. They look like more for the money. That is the trend in design today—massiveness—in automobiles, in everything you buy."

Another speaker says:

"Without use of trickery or artifice, to prove my point I show these figures."

Let's take a shot at that:

"Here are some figures. They are from the United States Census. No trickery, no fooling—they're the McCoy. And do they prove my point?"

I also heard this one:

"Having wandered pretty far afield, permit me to get back to my subject."

Okay, Bud, who's holding you back? But let's see what we can do for that one.

"Let's get back to the subject."

In a case like that, it might be better to sneak back without any reference to the fact that you wandered all around the half acre.

Then there is the introductory phrase that tries to pack all the ideas into it. Here is one I noted:

"From this basic consideration of economy of purchase and use, this appliance is a good buy."

Why not write that:

"This appliance is a good buy. It is a good buy any way you look at it—low price—low cost of operation."

Just analyze that for speaking effectiveness. You emphasize "good buy," "low price," "low cost of operation." True wording has helped some in that emphasis but arrangement has had its share in the improvement.

Too often the speaker may bury his main idea in that opening phrase. Or he may overpower the main idea with an opening phrase that has only minor importance.

Usually you will do better if you write the idea in the opening phrase as a sentence that stands on its own feet. Then you have a chance to look at it and judge it on its merits. Perhaps you will discard it entirely. If it does not help the idea, it is better to give it the blue pencil. In most cases, the separate sentence improves the speech. For instance, a speaker says, "If you have read your newspaper in the last few weeks—." Write that "In the last few weeks the newspapers have been full of—."

Here is another case:

> At the risk of oversimplifying a problem as difficult and complex as advertising I would suggest, in an effort to be helpful, the following formula, which will work, I venture to say, for at least some of you.

I did not write that statement. It was taken from a speech. But let's see how we can express that idea in spoken rather than written words. As you look over that interminable sentence, remember that each mark of punctuation made a separate sentence when the sentence was spoken. It is written as one long sentence but it is spoken as a number of small sentences, and if the speaker does not stick too closely to the written text it might sound all right. But let's revise it to get rid of that opening clause:

> Advertising is difficult and complex. It can't be simplified too much. But here is a formula that might help some of you.

There are twenty-two words in that revision instead of the thirty-nine in the original; three sentences instead of one. Perhaps some of the meaning is lost, but I doubt that enough is lost to make any difference to the audience. Remember that they do not get exact meanings anyway.

All these examples tend to prove the point that it is better to talk directly. So let's write directly.

In the past few years I have gone over a number of scripts for speeches and have cut out all the written words and written forms. It is amazing how these deletions and the substitution of spoken words have improved the pieces as talking scripts. In my work I have to look over scripts for training films. Conscientiously I edit out what I consider written words or forms. Then in the revision of these scripts the expressions and words creep back in again. That is because script writers are writers first and perhaps not talkers at all. You couldn't expect a man to say "the crisp, crunchy, aromatic goodness." Yet those are good written words. I assume so because advertisers pay good money to have such copy appear in print. In fact those words came out of an advertisement in a leading magazine.

Now what are the points to watch on spoken versus written language? Let's sum up:

1. Since you have to speak the speech, stick to spoken words.
2. Try for the simplest words to help the audience to understand. Not "annually," use "every year"; not "daily," use "every day."
3. Remember you can't spell out each involved word. The listeners must understand it as you say it.
4. If you are a writer you will probably have a more difficult

time writing your speeches. You know too many words and word tricks.

5. Dodge adjectives—particularly those double and triple headers that advertising men go for.

6. Watch those dangling phrases, "assuring," etc. They don't belong in spoken language.

7. Shy clear of negative words. Say it positively.

8. Remember the audience must hear and understand in the time it takes you to say the word.

The best way to understand this difference between spoken and written words is to listen to speeches. When you don't understand a word or phrase, make a note of it. That is how I have come by most of the ideas expressed here. They are not theories. A speaker said something that I didn't understand. I made a note of what he said and when I checked back I found that most the troubles came because the speaker was using the writer's tricks—trying to get in all the ideas without using enough words to express the ideas fully.

9. Write It in Units

Writing your speech in units will save you time. It will result in a better speech. You have a synopsis and the material has been laid out on paper, in squares, as suggested in Chap. 3. Now as you look over that layout, what suggests itself? The material breaks up into a number of parts, doesn't it—parts or units. So let's write this talk in units.

A unit will be much like a short speech. It will be a short speech that covers one of the parts of your longer speech. You write a number of smaller speeches, you put them together, and you have a long speech.

There are a number of advantages in writing a speech this way.

1. You concentrate your thinking on one unit at a time and you plan and organize that unit more completely. You are not bothered by a score of ideas that belong in other units. By working out one idea only, an idea that will take you three or four minutes to express, you give it more complete coverage.

2. The outline for a complete speech is a real chore, but the outline for one unit is not too difficult to make. At home tonight you lay out and assemble the notes on a unit. What points do you want to make? What data do you have to make those points? What data do you have to look up? Tomorrow at the office you use the outline to dictate the unit to the girl or the machine.

3. You are not overwhelmed at the thought of writing a thirty-minute speech. You are doing a three- or four-minute unit. Think of the times you have put off writing that speech. You had to take a day off or give up a whole Sunday. And you sent the wife and kids off to Grandma's while you went to it. Nighttime found you

completely exhausted, not too satisfied with your efforts, and swearing you'd have your head examined if anyone ever again talked you into writing a speech. Well, those days are gone forever.

4. You can write a unit at odd times. A few notes on the back of an envelope while you are waiting for a customer, while you are on the train or the bus, or those few minutes tonight before the neighbors show up to play bridge. Always you can find the time to outline a three- or four-minute unit.

5. By writing in units, you can better appraise the point made by that unit. Perhaps it is not worth a unit when you get all the evidence assembled. Many times a point that seems important when you start to write the speech boils itself down to a mere statement without much to back it up. When that happens under this plan, the evidence can be combined in another unit or discarded.

6. Under this writing-by-units plan, you have a talk that can be cut to almost any length. If the complete talk runs to thirty minutes, you can cut it to twenty by eliminating units. You don't have to go through the whole speech and cut out some part of each unit. You eliminate one or more units completely. Since you give each point complete coverage, the audience will never know that you have cut anything.

When you get the units written in the first rough form you can then start to assemble the parts to see how they fit together. Now you may have to do some revising. The illustration that you used in one unit may be too similar to one used in another unit. Your synopsis and your layout on paper will prevent most of this overlapping, but still you will find some of it in the completed speech.

If we followed the unit idea in the speech on "How to Run a Sales Meeting," the one we laid out on paper in Chap. 3, we would have separate units on—

1. Definition	5. Fumbling
2. Use of Room	6. Use of Charts
3. Variety	7. Audience Participation
4. Interest	8. Competition
9. Ending	

Each unit would be built on a simple plan. First, state the point you are to make. Second, bring out the illustrations that help make the point. Third, sum up by restating the point. In the unit covering "Use of Room," you want the audience to think about the room in which the meeting is to be held and how it can best be used for a successful meeting. You tell them that the room is important to the success of the meeting. Then you give the details about the type of room to select, the shape that is best. Explain why the entrance should be in the rear, suggest the seating arrangements, compare the room arrangement they should have with that of a theater. Explain what to do about the chairman, about a head table, and about the position of the speaker and his props. In doing this you discuss the room in which you are speaking. Tell what is good about it, what is wrong about it. They know this room. Perhaps they meet in it every week.

Mentioning the room in which the meeting is held is good speaking technique, but I must point out that my coverage of this point in a talk to the Rotary Club of my home town got me in bad with the local hotel help. The meeting was held in the hotel ballroom and the head table was placed in front of a row of street windows. I told the club that such an arrangement was wrong because it left the audience looking at the windows. Always the audience should be seated with its back toward the windows. The next week the club tried to have the room arranged as I suggested. The hotel help argued. The club explained that I had suggested it. Then the help ganged up on me.

After you have covered the points given above, you restate your premise that the room and the room arrangement are important. That makes your unit on the room. Each of the other eight units in the talk might be handled in the same way.

Some units in your talk will break down into bits that can be used as a separate talk. Time and again I have used the unit above as a three-minute talk, complete in itself. I don't imagine that the audiences realized that it was only part of a longer speech, but it has most of the elements of a good speech. It presents an idea, it gives illustrations that support the idea, it restates the idea. Of course I

need an introduction and a better ending for this short speech, but
these can be handled in two or three sentences that lead me into and
out of the subject. As an introduction for this unit I usually say a
few words about the training of the trainers. I state that trainers
need to be trained in simple things. "Take the meeting room," I
continue. "Who has ever taught the men who put on your meetings
how much the arrangement of the meeting room can help a meeting?" With such an introduction I can launch into my unit. In three
minutes I have given the audience some ideas and I am done. For
my finish I use, "First, select the best room you can get, and second, arrange it to help your meeting." That presents an easy-to-
remember two-step plan to follow.

Since it is always well to be prepared with a few well-chosen
words if you are called on to speak, writing a speech in units can be
a lifesaver. There are parts in almost every long speech that can be
used in this way.

To give you a better idea of how a unit is built, here is a formula
for you. This formula I got the hard way, by sitting in meetings,
listening to good speakers, and making notes. I can guarantee that
it is sure-fire.

1. State the premise.
2. Quote an ancient.
3. Quote a poet.
4. Quote the Bible.
5. Tell an anecdote about a famous character.
6. Tell a story about an ordinary character.
7. Wind up with a second statement of your premise.

You don't need all these elements to make a good unit. You might
use three or four. One alone can help make your point. You may
state your premise, use one quotation, one story about an ordinary
character, then repeat your premise. Those four parts would make
a unit. That may be enough for a two-minute talk. When you have
more time you might bring in another one of the elements. All of
them are sure-fire. Of course, some speakers don't go in for quoting
ancients, or poets, or even the Bible. That's perfectly all right.

Others don't have a pat story to tell about a famous character. That's all right, too.

The above list of the seven parts of an elaborate unit should give you a better idea of what is meant by a unit. Now let's discuss each of these elements.

STATE THE PREMISE—Tell them what you're going to tell them, like the Negro preacher. Let's say your premise is, "It Pays to Smile." Tell them that it pays to smile. Tell them once, then tell them again in slightly different words.

QUOTE AN ANCIENT—Yes, quote Socrates, Plato, Marcus Aurelius, Cato, Homer—any known person who lived long ago. Few in the audience will know the quotation you select, so you can change it a bit to prove your point. Quoting the ancient on your premise shows that your idea was a good one thousands of years ago. This kind of quotation is especially good for the professional man who feels it is good advertising to present some evidence of education.

QUOTE A POET—Bring in Shakespeare, Emerson, Longfellow, Robert Service, James Whitcomb Riley, Edgar Guest—on your premise, of course. What did they say about the value of a smile? It makes little difference which one you quote so long as he is known. Again, you are dealing with the unfamiliar. Most people won't know the quotation; thus it will come as a new idea to them.

QUOTE THE BIBLE—All will agree with what that Good Book says about the value of a smile. Maybe Plato or Longfellow didn't register, but the Bible is sure-fire. Everybody will agree; at least they won't stand up in a meeting and argue with you.

TELL AN ANECDOTE ABOUT A FAMOUS CHARACTER—This will have to be strong, for remember that you are building up. What this character said about a smile must be good. You may have to take a story you have heard and change it to suit your purpose. Let's say that there are two million Lincoln stories now. The world is not going to fall apart because you devise Story number Two Million and One.

STORY ABOUT AN ORDINARY PERSON—Here you bring in the type of person you associate with every day—a taxi driver, a newsdealer, your wife or kids. This happened to you today, to an ordinary person—you. Always place yourself in this final story. Always give that personal experience which shows how once it paid you to smile.

Note the time sequence in this formula for a unit. You start with long ago and far away and build right up to today. That's good technique. It is something like the "past, present, future" formula. The ancient, the poet, the Bible—those all build background for you. But the audience doesn't quite understand them. They're beyond the experience of most persons. Even when you bring in the famous character you are on unfamiliar ground, for few persons in your audience know any of the famous. But the story about you and the taxi driver—ah, now you're talking our language. We know you, we know the taxi driver.

Here is an example of how to use all seven of these elements in building a unit.

UNIT FOR A SPEECH

(Following the seven-step formula)

Title: "It Pays To Smile"

1. State the premise

A smile pays. It paid one man one million dollars per year. When Charles Schwab, the steel man, was asked what contributed most to his success, what did he answer? He didn't give the credit to his knowledge of the steel business, nor to his ability or his physique. No sir, not one of them. His answer was, "My smile." He was one of the greatest salesmen that the world has known, if not the greatest, and he said his smile was his greatest asset. His company paid him one million dollars per year salary. For his smile. Yet, the trouble with most of us is that we forget to smile. I walk into a store. Are the salesclerks glad to see me? I have no way of telling unless they smile at me and most times they do not smile. They seem covered over by their own worries. They don't seem friendly and I don't feel too much like buying. I go into church. Nobody smiles at me and I feel that I am a stranger. Smile at me and I am more likely to do business with you. Smile and I feel as if I belong. Yes, the smile wins. A smile pays big dividends. Always it pays you to smile.

2. Quote an ancient. (Don't hold me to these quotes. I'm simply using them as examples.)

Marcus Aurelius said, "The man with a smile makes friends." Now isn't that true? Think of the person you like best. I mean outside your immediate family. Isn't one of his big characteristics his smile? How much of your liking for him comes because of that smile?

Writers always put it, "A smile lights up his face." You never read a passage that told you a smile darkened a character's face. Perhaps a sneer, or a leer, or a smirk. But never a smile. A smile lights up your face, the customer's face, a friend's face, and if you're in business it might change those little numbers on the cash register. You have had that happen to you. I was standing on a street corner in Los Angeles waiting for a bus. A voice said, "Mister, your shoes could do with a shine." I looked at my shoes. They didn't need a shine. I had brushed them with that little flannel cloth in my hotel room not ten minutes before. I looked at the boy who owned the voice. He was smiling up at me. I smiled back. "Okay," I said, and put my foot on his little box. The need for a shine had not made that sale. It was the boy's smile. A smile does things like that to you.

3. Quote a poet. (Why not the Bard himself? Don't look up the quote.)

Shakespeare said, "Smile and the world smiles with you. Weep and you weep alone." You have no time for the fellow who is a sourpuss. Nobody wants to do business with him. Nobody wants to associate with him. I have my own troubles. You have yours. I don't want yours, you don't want mine. On the other hand, you admire the fellow who laughs off his troubles and who seems to be cheerful no matter what. Weep if you want to, but you will have to hunt longer for a shoulder to weep on.

4. Quote the Bible

The Bible says, "A soft answer turneth away wrath." A smile does that too. How can a man be mean to you if you take it with such good grace that you smile at him? When you smile you indicate you want to be friends. Perhaps you stepped on his foot in a crowd or crossed him in some way. You might have said, "Pardon me." But if you smile while you apologize, your statement means much more to him.

The other day I was looking through the index of one of those success books. You know the kind that advises a young man how to succeed. And what word do you think got the most mention in the index? Work—that's right.

Work was mentioned twenty-two times. Sweat ten times. Effort nine times. Thinking thirteen times and smiling fourteen times. Think of that! Smiling before thinking or effort or sweat. Only work got more mention than a smile. And the man who works and smiles too is on top of the world.

If Lincoln could smile at a humorous joke or a cartoon even with the weight of the troubles of the Union upon him, why should we go around with grouches over our petty inconveniences? The day's mile can be shortened by prefixing an "s" to it and making it "smile."

5. Anecdote about a famous character

F.D.R. had a famous smile. His enemies spoke of his great personal charm. Always in cartoon and caricature he was pictured with his smile— a long cigarette holder and a smile. That smile was an asset, one that won him friends and got him votes. One of my friends was a bitter anti-New Dealer, anti-Democrat, anti-Roosevelt.

One day he was called down to the White House as a member of a trade committee. He came away still anti-everything. But not the committee.

"F.D.R. swayed the committee. He wrapped them up and tied them with a string," my friend said. "He's got charm, that fellow. And back of it all is that damnable smile. Somehow it gets you." His smile made friends, got votes, and won over his enemies to work for him. You know a sincere smile is a rare thing.

The teacher asked little Johnnie, "Johnnie, can you tell me what a hypocrite is?"

Johnnie answered that one fast. "I think so," he said. "It's a boy who comes to school with a smile on his face."

6. Story about an ordinary character

Yes, a sincere smile is a rare thing. It lightens up your whole day. I was walking up the ramp from the Cleveland Union Station one day. A large, fat fellow stopped me. After greeting me he said, "You're the first fellow who has come along here in the last ten minutes without a frown on his face. Why is everybody frowning?" I looked at the fellow. I had never seen him before, but his smile indicated that he was regular and that he would make a good friend to have. "I don't know," I told him. "I guess they are worrying about the ills of the world." It was the best I could think of at the moment. "That's the trouble with the world," he said. "Everybody's frowning. Let's stand and watch." Well, I stood there with him watching.

Everybody hurrying by had a frown on his or her face. "Why no smiles?" my friend kept murmuring, and I couldn't answer. Since that day I have stood on streets, in hotels, in railway stations, watching the crowds go by. Seldom do I see a smile. The man with a smile stands out in a crowd of people you don't know, just as he stands out among the persons you know.

And why don't more of us smile? It's easier than frowning. It takes only five facial muscles to smile. It takes almost three times as many—fourteen—to frown. And yet more people frown than smile. There is no sense in it.

7. Wind-up. Restate the premise

If you have any doubt that a smile makes friends, just try smiling. Remember, you don't feel friendly to a man who looks like a grouch. Smile, then watch your smile transfer to other faces. It's a thrill. Light your face with a smile and you brighten the world around you. You make friends and you prove to yourself that a smile pays—with friends, with business, and with yourself. The poem puts it very well:

> It's easy enough to be pleasant
> When the world runs along like a song
> But the man worthwhile is one who can
>   smile
> When everything goes dead wrong.

Yes, a smile pays. It paid Charlie Schwab. It pays the salesperson in the store. It pays the man who owns the store. And it will pay you. Try it, please. Tomorrow morning when you first get up, smile at that fellow in the mirror. Smile at the girl who gets your breakfast. Smile at the first ten people you meet. You'll make your day brighter. And you will help all those others too.

That shows how a unit can be built. If you happen to need a ten-minute speech sometime, try this one. I'll bet it will go over well, for it has all the elements that make for a good speech. It could be improved by better illustrations, and some research might bring out better quotations; remember that I said I authored some of those

quotations and tied them up with a good name. But what I was trying to do was to give you an illustration of how a unit is built.

The unit plan will save time and worry in your speech writing.
It will give you better organization. When you have the units written, you can arrange them in the best speech order. Here again are
some of the advantages of this "unit at a time" idea:

1. You confine your thoughts to one small part of the speech.
2. You write only one small part at a time. The "It Pays to
   Smile" example runs only about 1400 words.
3. Your material usually breaks up into units. Certain points in
   the speech seem to belong together.
4. You strengthen the points by giving them individual treatment.
5. You give each point complete coverage.
6. You button up each thought in its own unit. There are no
   loose ends. The audience knows what you are getting at and,
   what's more, you do too.
7. You can outline a unit in odd moments—when you are waiting for the bus, or the friends, or the wife, or the girl friend.
   But don't try to keep the outline in your head. Write it
   down.
8. When you have the units written you can check one against
   the other for similarity of ideas or illustrations.
9. You can appraise the point the unit makes. If it is not strong
   enough, you can build it up or discard it.
10. The unit plan allows you to cut the talk to any length. You
    don't worry about revising. You leave out one or more units.
11. After the units are done you can shuffle them in the order
    that makes the best speech.
12. With a number of these units on hand you are always pre-
    pared to make a few choice remarks on your favorite subject.

Now that you are familiar with the unit plan, let's write the first
unit. Which one will it be? Why, the end, of course.

10. Write the End First

Now that we have the synopsis and layout and have discussed the language to use, let's write the end of our speech first. Since we are writing the speech in units, it makes no difference what part you write first.

Starting with the end has a number of advantages. Not long ago I heard a speaker wind up his story with, "As I said when I started, I didn't know what to tell you in ten minutes. But I've told you this —I think that's all I've got to say." Can't you picture the audience sitting on its hands after that ending? Can't you imagine the deflated feeling of the speaker? He had been asked to talk. He had prepared a speech but in the time available he could only organize the start and the body of his speech; he never got around to the ending. Now if he had prepared a good ending, I'm sure the audience would have thought better of him. No matter how good your speech, if you end like a slow leak, you are certain to leave a bad impression.

Your speech should have a good ending because that is where you sum up, restate your main theme, or give the audience the information on what they are to do.

A well-shaped ending gives you confidence. If you write the beginning of the speech first, you are certain to put most of your ideas up in front. Then you run out of ideas and wonder where you will go from there. That's the weakness of most of the speeches you hear. They start at top speed. At the high point, the audience is won over and is ready to do something. But as the speaker goes on, the enthusiasm of the group goes down, down, down, until at the finish the enthusiasm which had been built up earlier has been completely dissipated. By writing the end first you can prevent that.

Your audience will be more impressed if you end your speech by giving them some kind of formula for action. If you want them to do something, to study something, to think about something, give them a formula for doing it. When you leave a formula with them it is apparent that you have thought out this project of yours and that you know exactly what you want them to do. Second, you make clear to them exactly what you want.

The formula may be a simple plan of greeting, no more complicated than—

1. You smile.
2. You offer your hand.
3. You say, "Howdy."

Just as simple as that. Such formulas never fail. Take the story you want the audience to remember, the job you want them to do, the something you want them to think about, and put the action into the steps of a simple formula. Make it as simple as the one above and you'll get more of them to do what you want.

That's because you specify the job. You pin it down. Many times you have heard people talk for hours, trying to get you steamed up about a subject. When they finished you were willing to do something, but they didn't tell you how. So you went home, thinking that you'd like to do something about it but not knowing where to start. They didn't give you a formula.

In writing the formula, first explain that there is one. Give it and list the steps. Then name the first point, elaborate on it, and explain fully what they are to do and how.

Go on to your second point. Follow the same plan in explaining that.

Then give step number three, handling it the same way. As you finish, repeat the three points.

Some of the best speeches you have heard ended with such a formula. You listened to them and you went away convinced that you had something to do, for the man had told you exactly how to do it. Such formulas are sure-fire speech material. They help you organize the subject. And they help keep it organized in the mind of the listener as he sits there listening. So let's give the audience a formula. Here are some suggestions that may help:

A sales manager might tell a group of salesmen: Here is what to do—it's easy—it's simple.

1. Call on ten stores this week.
2. Show the product and explain the deal.
3. Ask for the order.

A speaker for a cause might finish:

1. Send a postcard to your congressman.
2. Write a letter to three friends, asking them to do the same.
3. Telephone three local friends and ask them to send a postcard.

A speaker for a fund drive might finish:

1. Call on your ten prospects.
2. Go through the fund circular with them.
3. Ask each to contribute ten dollars.

Get the idea? Make your formula as simple as you can. Don't list too many points. More than three points becomes confusing. Maybe you need four steps for this deal you are presenting. Perhaps five. But don't go beyond five. It's difficult for people to remember that many steps. Keep the steps down to three and you'll get more of your audience to follow the ones you suggest.

But let's get on with the writing. First, write on a piece of paper the points you want to make in your summation. If you want to tell them what to do and how to do it, write that down. In my talk on the sales meeting, I want the audience to realize that most of the training of sales people who sell their goods is given in sales meetings. I want to impress that point on them. Next I want them to put on better sales meetings. My story on that, in a three-step ending, is:

1. Teach your sales people to put on better meetings. If you do, you'll—

2. Have better trained salesmen who will sell more goods, and
3. Because you sell more goods you'll keep a few more men working at your factories.

The three points tell the audience what they are to do and why they should do it. It's a bit wordy, for a real bang-up ending, so let's shorten it:

1. Put on better training meetings.
2. Your salesmen will sell more.
3. You'll have more men working at your factory.

That ending is brief, it is fast, you can say it quickly and sit down. It will make a good last paragraph, but it is not a complete ending. Let's look at the chart layout on this talk and see what we collected for the ending:

Don't let end flicker out
Recess before end
Write end first
Story of man called upon without idea
The three-step ending
Finally—in conclusion

Let's start writing from those notes and see what we have.

Mark Twain tells a story about a preacher and his sermon. When the speaker had been going for five minutes, Mark was willing to drop two dollars in the collection plate. When the preacher had been going for ten minutes he was willing to put out a dollar. When the sermon had been going for thirty minutes, he felt that the preacher owed him money.

Five minutes, two dollars; ten minutes, one dollar; thirty minutes, not a red cent. That's the way it is with so many meetings.

One way to keep from owing the audience money is to plan the end of the meeting first. That may sound like putting the cart before the horse, but it can make good sense, for the finish is most likely to give the impression the listeners take home. Some speakers write the end of their speeches first and then go back and build the start and the middle up to that end. The same plan can be used for the end of your meeting.

Always there is some idea you want to sell or something you want the audience to do. Ask yourself, "What do I want to sell?" or "What do I want them to do and how will they do it?"

The answer to those two questions will give you a clear picture of what you want to cover in that end. If you are selling an idea, you may want to cover it at the start of the speech, but don't forget to bring it in again at the end. They are more likely to remember it if you bring it up again just before they go home. If you are assigning a task, tell them what they are to do, and why and how, and give them any other information they need. If at the end of the meeting you are talking about what the group is to do and how it is to do it, they leave you knowing.

You have all heard the chairman of your club put one of the brothers on the spot by asking him to say a few words on some club project. Slowly brother so-and-so gets to his feet. He starts in a low voice. He ums and ahs. He is off his base and it is quite apparent to all in the meeting that he is up the creek without the proper equipment, but bravely and futilely he goes on. Finally he reaches the point where he feels that he has done his duty by the club and the chairman and he ends lamely, "Well, fellows, that's all I got to say." Too many meetings end like that. "Well, that's it, boys, any questions?" Many times they add, "If not, I'll be glad to buy you all a beer." It's just like Porky Pig lisping, "That's all, folks."

Now I'm going to give you a tip that will make you seem like a smart fellow when the chairman puts you on the spot with a request that you say a few words on one of the club projects, to which you have given little or no thought. The usual procedure is to out with an envelope and start making notes of what you'll say. Now it's okay to make the notes, but not on what you'll say—make them only on your ending. Don't worry about what you'll say at any time except in that minute before you sit down. On that envelope write—

What you must remember to do, say, tell others (use the one that fits) about this matter is—

First, this
Second, this
Third, this

Now sit down and you have left a good impression.

So when the chairman says that he is going to call upon you for a few remarks, don't try to figure out what you are going to say during the start of the speech. If you try to work out a complete speech, you won't get it done. But you almost always have time to work out a three-step finish. Get that end worked out. Then when you are called, get up slowly, start on the low beat. Um and ah as much as you want in the start and middle of your remarks. Then when you have taken up the time you think you should, throw your three-step plan at them—

First, go jump in the lake.
Second, swim out.
Third, hang your clothes up to dry.

Now sit down and the crowd will say, "That guy surely knows his stuff." You'll be surprised at the number of members who will compliment you on your remarks. You're the same fellow—old Mac without an idea—but your organized ending will make you seem like a new Mac.

Why, just last week I got a letter from a fellow who heard me make this speech and give this suggestion. He wrote, "Hegarty, that's a swell suggestion. I tried it out last week in a meeting of one of my clubs. I didn't have an idea on the subject when the president told me he would call on me. I didn't try to think up any either. I took your tip and concentrated on a three-step ending. Did it work? Brother, I wowed them. So much so that they appointed me chairman of the committee to carry out the project. Mr. Hegarty, if you have any more suggestions like that—well, I'm too much of a gentleman to tell you what to do with them."

That's gratitude for you. But it shows that the suggestion works. Try it next time.

Don't bring your audience to the end of your meeting dead tired. If you are assigning a job in that ending, give them a recess just before the end—perhaps ten or fifteen minutes. Then when they come back refreshed, assign the task.

One of my friends says, "Always I have a good ending to my

speeches. Then if the place catches on fire when I am half finished, I can bring out my end and wind up as I planned to." He was joking, but he did have a point. Many times you are in a spot where you want to wind up your meeting in a hurry. If you have a good ending, you can bring it out when you see it is time to stop.

I am spending this much time on the ending because the finish is usually the weak part of the sales meeting. You can do a lot to make the end of your meetings better, and you can do even more to make the whole of your sales meetings better. You have seen everything I have talked about today happen in meetings; you have seen most of it happen in your own meetings. It is easy to correct these meeting faults. I say that because I have tried. I have worked with men who put on meetings one at a time and with groups of them, and the improvement that these men showed in their presentations was amazing. You can do that too. Work with your men who put on meetings, teach them how to do this job, and you too will be surprised at the results. The fellow who can't speak for sour apples becomes a better speaker. The one who fumbles does things easily. The one who seemed uncertain gives the appearance of an expert. These fellows don't make mistakes because they want to. They do it because they don't know better. And since you're the boss, it's your job to teach them to do better.

Such instruction will pay off handsomely for you. When you consider that most of the training of salesmen who sell your goods is done in sales meetings, it doesn't take a mathematician to see that if you—

1. Put on better sales meetings,
2. Your salesmen will sell more, and
3. You'll have more men working at the factory.

There is an ending that ends. It can no doubt be improved, but it gives you an example. It is an ending that I have used forty or fifty times, changing it a bit now and then to suit conditions. Note that I don't say "finally" or "in conclusion" in any part of it. Don't tell them you are going to end. Sneak up on them with that ending. Let your story build up logically to that end, but don't tell them that you will be finished in a few minutes. Surprise them— they like it.

With that end written, the balance of the speech may be changed a bit so that it builds up to the end. Note that the philosophy of the speech is stated at the end—the big selling point is brought out here so that the audience will remember it. It is the idea I want them to take home, so I place it where they will be most likely to remember it.

Now let's review the points that have been made:

1. The ending gives the impression the audience takes home. For that reason it should be good.
2. The end of your speech is where you sum up. Make sure that you do sum up in your ending.
3. If you want the audience to do something, write out the instructions and use them for the ending.
4. The formula is good for the ending. Give the audience a formula—first, this; second, that; third, the other.
5. When you wind up with a formula, use as few steps as possible.
6. Get the habit of using the three-step-formula ending for the extemporaneous speech.
7. Don't write "finally" or "in conclusion" in your ending. Let your ending sneak up on the audience.
8. Don't wind up with the perennial "Thank you." Make your words finish for you.
9. Put what you want them to remember, what you want them to do, in that end.

11. Start with a Smile

SMILE!

That's the first word you'll write at the beginning of this talk of yours. Write it down in capital letters. It isn't a word you'll speak; it's a stage direction.

Sounds silly, doesn't it? But here's why you start your talk with a smile. After the introduction, speaker after speaker stands up and scowls at his audience. Others simply try to look dignified. Just picture the situation. Here you stand before the group, a total stranger. If you scowl at the audience, they scowl back at you. If you try to look dignified, they groan inwardly and sit back expecting the worst. But if you smile, your smile transfers itself to their faces and, brother, you're off to a head start.

But this is to be a serious speech, you say. Maybe so, but you're glad to be there, aren't you? Yes, with your knees knocking together and your throat constricted, you're still glad to be there. And so you smile. You must write it down at the start of your speech so that, first, you'll remember it, and second, you'll plan just how you will smile.

Perhaps at this moment, as you are writing the beginning of your speech, you may see little to smile about. But there will be plenty. Why, when you stand up to speak, you'll have just heard the chairman introduce you. That's good for a smile always, perhaps a laugh. To you, anyway, his verbal efforts to convince people that he has brought a real big number to talk to them should be good for a smile. And if he gave no better break than to say you were a brother-in-law of Mr. X, who happened to be in town, you can smile at that. You can smile at the things he should have said but didn't. Yes, you can smile at what he said and at what he left out.

Then you can smile about what you thought when they first asked you to make this speech. Now you're there looking at the group to whom you are to talk. Think back to what you thought about them when you received the invitation. That should be good for a smile, for never are they what you imagined.

Just to show you what a smile does to the audience, I am going to give you a demonstration that I give to audiences. I have a chart with the illustration you will see below. There is nothing on this chart but the circle and the curved line. Keeping the chart covered, I say, "I want to give you a demonstration of the value of a smile. Now I want you to look intently at this chart—all of you—look intently at this chart." When I have full attention I show the illustration. Try it, please; look intently at this illustration for ten seconds.

You are now smiling. That illustration isn't a complete face. It is just an outline with a line to represent a mouth. But you are smiling back at it. Now if I can get you to smile with a simple drawing on a sheet of paper, think what you can do with a friendly smile when you face your audience.

So start by writing it down. Make it the first word. Get it right up there at the top of the first page, even before the "Ladies and gentlemen—." Make it such an important part of your talk that you can't forget it.

If you get up there without a plan for that smile, you may forget it. So write it down now.

SMILE

That will get you off to a good start.

12. Once upon a Time

Back three chapters I wrote a sample unit for you. How did it start? With a story, of course. Not a funny story, but an anecdote about Charles Schwab. That is a good way to start any speech. Tell an anecdote about the chairman of the meeting, the wife and kids, the persons in the hall. "Once upon a time" is always your best bet for a start.

In the days of vaudeville the monologist started with, "On my way over from the hotel. . . ." Today the radio comedian varies that to, "On my way to the studio tonight. . . ." Why? Because by telling a story he is catching and holding your interest. Few of us can resist the appeal of a story.

Any expert speaker uses stories to catch and hold your interest. They are his main stock in trade. Listen to any good speaker and, no matter what his subject, sooner or later he bobs up with an anecdote. He uses the story to make a point, to build up an idea, to bring back your lagging interest, and to do scores of other speaking jobs.

The story makes ordinary material more interesting. Not long ago I was helping a speaker with a speech. At one point he planned to describe a gadget that would help retail salespeople sell electric roasters. In his written talk he had this line, "This particular gadget will help you sell electric roasters."

There was nothing wrong with that line. What he said was true. The gadget had been used and it had helped make sales. But that statement—just nine words—didn't sound very impressive to me.

"How do you know that gadget will help them make sales?" I asked.

"Because a little redhead in the Newark store told me it sold three roasters for her last week."

"Why not tell it that way?" I asked. He did, and he increased interest in his gadget and also improved his chances of holding the attention of his audience. Both of those methods—the statement and the story—expressed the same thought, but how differently! And it's such differences that make one speech dull and another interesting.

How did he put his gadget into an anecdote? Well, here's how it could be done:

> The other day I was over in the Newark store. They told me that one of the salespeople had sold two roasters per day for the last two weeks. Now that was something—two per day for two weeks—and so I thought I'd look up this superman and see how the job was done. Well, my superman turned out to be a super-lady—a little redhead named Betsy. When I asked her how come, she showed me this little gadget. Now look at that (hold up gadget). Doesn't look like much, does it? But she told me that this gadget was the reason for her success. With it she had made that sales record. Here's how she used it. . . .

With that, the speaker demonstrates the gadget. Note how the anecdote plays up the gadget. It doesn't get sidetracked on the saleslady or her sales methods—it sticks to its point and focuses interest on the gadget.

That's what the anecdote should do. It should help you towards some objective. In opening an after-dinner talk I always try to start in a humorous vein. I talk to a lot of sales-executive clubs and usually a member of the club will take me aside before the dinner and explain how good the preceding speakers have been. And so I have a number of anecdotes about how the various clubs have needled me to try to get a good talk out of me. I start with one story about arriving in a town at six forty-five in the morning and being met by six members of the club. As each shook my hand, he said, "Ed, we're glad to have you down here. The last speaker we had was good."

I tell three such stories, then I tell what the member of the local club did to me. With those four stories I establish the fact that I am a regular fellow and that I am going to make a good speech. Since they like the stories I am telling, they feel they will like the speech too.

Even the stories that bring a laugh should help make a point. However, to this audience the story will be interesting whether or not it makes a point. I have one story I use to prove this point. I tell the story and they listen with interest. They even laugh when I finish my gag line. Then I tell them that the story made no point, yet they listened because it was a story.

I have a plan on these stories that may help get your point across:

1. State your point.
2. Tell your anecdote.
3. Restate your point.

In the story on the gadget that sold roasters, the speaker could say:

"This little gadget will help you sell electric roasters. I'm going to tell you why I know it will help you. . . ."

Now he tells the story about the little redhead. Then he restates his point.

"If that little lady can sell electric roasters by using this gadget, you can too."

The other day a friend was describing a speech he heard. "This fellow wasn't telling funny stories," he said. "He was making a point with every one of them. But he had that audience laughing almost continuously." I have heard speakers like that and so have you. They get laughs and make points.

Such stories are not difficult to find. This noon at lunch a man tells you something. Tonight when you go home and tell the wife what happened at lunch today, you are telling a story. When you start, "Today at lunch. . . ." she is all ears.

Perhaps the story you heard at lunch is not in the form which will help make a point for you, but you can put it into a form to make good speech material. Not long ago I was asked to talk to a group of college professors. Somewhere I had heard this definition of education, "The incompetent teaching the incomprehensible to the ignorant." I thought I might use that to start my speech. But to follow my rule of starting with a story, I built an anecdote around this line:

> When I was asked to make this speech to you today, I was a bit worried. Speaking to college professors isn't in my line. So I did what we always do around our shop when we're in a spot like that. I went to see a wise man. We have one of those in our place. One who knows the answers to everything. So I went to him, I told him my troubles, and he said: "There is no reason why you should be afraid of those people. Why, those college professors are just like anybody else. Don't you know what education is?" he asked.
>
> "No," I replied. "What is education?"
>
> "Simply the incompetent teaching the incomprehensible to the ignorant."

When you build a story around such a line, don't make the story too short. The line itself might have done for a starter, but it may have been said too fast for the group to get its meaning. Notice that even with the story I followed the method of the interlocutor in the minstrel show and repeated the question, "What is education?" That built up more interest in the last line.

Both of the anecdotes had a place in these talks. The first illustrated a point. The second built up a wisecrack that might have been lost had it been quoted as a definition. As you write your talk, you will have to spot stories such as these all through the script. You need them to hold interest. To prove this, check the next good talker you hear.

This means that you will have to analyze the material you have for story possibilities. If you have a wiscrack like the one about education, see how you can put it in story form. Usually you can't pick stories out of a newspaper or a book and use them as they are written. Stories printed in books are usually in written language. In the book, a line of conversation may read, " 'But that's not true!' he exclaimed, showing the first sign of irritation." You can't speak words like that. So if you were using a story written in that kind of language, you will have to revise it. Some such stories require a lot of revision, others can be changed easily. Let's show by an actual example what I mean. Here is a story picked out of a joke book. Let's say you want to use it. Here is how it appears in the book:

> "I think it's so exciting eating oyster stew," observed the conversational waiter to the diner. "There's always the chance you may find a pearl."
> "Humph!" growled the customer, poking about his bowl with his spoon, "I'll settle for an oyster."

Now what's wrong with that story as speech material? First, it is in written language. Second, it gives the diner the gag line.

Now let's put the story into a form that will go over well in a speech.

> The other day I went into a restaurant, sat down at a table, picked up the menu, and the first thing that struck my eye was oyster stew. That'll be just about right, I thought. When the waiter came I placed the order. The waiter went off, and soon he was back with the crackers and the hot stuff. Well, I was feeling expansive, it was a fine sunshiny day, and just to make conversation I said, "You know it's exciting to eat oyster stew. There's always the chance that you might find a pearl."
> The waiter looked at me without saying a word, then he smiled. "Why the smile?" I asked.
> He shook his head, "Brother, in the stew you get here, you'll be lucky to find an oyster."

Now it makes a good story for a speech. Note the changes I made. I cut "observed the conversational waiter," "growled the customer," "Humph!" "diner." Those changes were made to cut out expressions that could not be easily spoken. Another change I made was reversing the characters. When you tell a story you cannot be the hero. You must always figure as a goat. If there is a joke, let it be on you. When you tell a story in which you are the hero, you seem to the audience to be showing off. When you reverse the order and let the joke be on you, they feel you are a regular guy, one of them.

Note also that I put myself into the narrative. Now the story is something personal. By having this happen to me, I make the story much more effective than if it happened to a friend of mine. Always inject yourself into your stories. This is the number one rule of effective storytelling. Don't say it happened to a small boy; make it your son. If it is a lady, have it your wife. If your story pictures a woman bawling out her husband, have it your wife heckling you. The audience can picture you. As you tell the story you are certain to take on the facial expressions you would if this action were happening to you. When the story is about you, you can't help acting out the experience for them to see. So put yourself into your stories.

Not long ago I heard a young priest do a sermon. His technique was:

1. Tell a story that made a point.
2. Button up the point.
3. Repeat one and two.

It was a good technique. He kept everybody's interest by telling a story that made a point. Then he would repeat the point and stress it. But the stressing lasted only for a few sentences. When he saw that they tired of his stressing, he switched to another point-making story.

This young man had learned that people will listen to stories. There are so many stories all around you. Something happens in the barbershop, or on the bus, or on the train—all these are interesting speech material. Shape them to your needs. Tell them in a way that helps prove your point. And your group will always listen, for from the time they were little kids they have not been able to resist the appeal of "Once upon a time. . . ."

The anecdote is about the most useful speaking tool you have. The story can be used to make ordinary material interesting. So practice using stories to make points. Do it in conversation, in conferences. You will find that the anecdote holds interest where the same material handled in other ways may not make much impression at all.

Now let's review the points made in this chapter.

1. Stories hold interest even though they don't make a point that advances the objective of the speech. You have heard the speaker who tells a funny story that has no relation at all to the point he is discussing. Avoid that, if you have the will power. It takes a strong man.

2. Give the story a job. See that the story makes your point. If it brings a laugh, consider that a plus. If the laugh overshadows the point, switch to another story that makes the point, perhaps without a laugh.

3. Don't write the story so short that the audience will not understand it. Elaborate on it, write it longer.

4. Be sure that the story is not in written language. Next time you read a joke in a newspaper you will see what I mean. You may smile at the wording in the newspaper, but if you use that wording before an audience, listeners will feel that you have memorized the gag. A man who says, "I would like to relate an incident . . . ," is asking for it.

5. If there is a butt in the story, let it be you. The audience likes the character who is the butt of jokes. Look at the popularity of Jack Benny.

6. Wherever possible put yourself in all the stories you tell. Don't tell what happened to a friend of yours or an acquaintance or a neighbor. Even if it did happen to one of them, when you tell the story, have it happen to you.

13. Sprinkle with Conversation

Another device for holding interest is conversation. It is usually so close to the anecdote that it is difficult to tell where one starts and the other leaves off. If I tell you that last Friday in Cleveland I saw this and that in a store window, you listen because I am telling a story. If I tell you that I went inside and spoke to the salesperson, you are again all ears because you want to hear what the clerk said to me and what I said to him. Invariably when you tell your friend that you told your wife something, his question is, "And what did she say?"

Gossip is a big business in the United States today. Columnists in the newspapers make a fine living reporting what she said to me and what I said to her. They write bits about a personality of whom you may or may not have heard. Yet because they write a friendly kind of gossip they have millions of readers. You have always heard that what the people say over the back-yard fence can win an election or build up the sales of a product. Play on that. You'll have a better speech if you write some gossipy conversation into it. Report what she said to you and your reply. What Max said to Louie and Louie's comeback. Your audience likes to listen to such dialogue.

In my speech, "How to Run a Sales Meeting," I use the story to prove the value of such dialogue in holding interest. Here is the story as it was written into the speech and as it has been told scores of times.

> I have a boy sixteen and last summer he got a job with the ice company. I don't know whether or not the boss told him about reciprocity, but he got into the habit of eating his lunch in the

88

bars and grills to which he delivered his ice. Before long he got so that he knew which bars had roast beef on which days and he got to know all the men who ran the places. Well, on this particular day he went into the place selected, sat himself at the bar, and ordered his lunch. It was a little before noon and the place was empty except for a drunk who was sitting in one of the booths, working on a crossword puzzle in the morning newspaper.

The boy had just about started on his lunch when the drunk lifted his head and called to the bartender, "Hey, Joe, what's a three-letter word that means wamph?"

Without turning his head, the boy called, "Wamph!"

The drunk wrote that down and a few minutes later he again called, "Hey, Joe, what's a four-letter word that means "Smalf?"

Without turning, the boy called, "Smalf."

The drunk wrote that in and was silent for a few minutes, filling in other spaces; then again he called, "Hey, Joe, what's a five-letter word that means "Mulku?"

A third time without turning, the boy called "Mulku."

It was too much for the drunk. He lifted his head, he shook himself, and called, "Hey, kid, if you're so damn smart, why you peddlin' ice?"

Now there is a story with no point at all. I call this to the attention of the audience after I have told the story. I tell them, "I have held your interest all through the telling of the story. Why? Because gossipy conversation interests you; you want to hear what the drunk said, what the boy said, and what Joe said."

That gives you an example of how to use conversation. Let's get on with some of the points we have to consider when such small talk is written into a speech. Perhaps the first rule is that it should take you somewhere. A conversation like the following gets nowhere fast.

"Hello."

"How're ya?"

"OK, and you?"

"So, so."

"You're lookin' good."

"So're you."

"Well, glad I saw you."

"Likewise."

Sounds something like Danny Kaye, but it doesn't prove any-thing except that some persons can do a lot of gabbing and not say anything. If you were trying to prove that persons can use a lot of words without saying anything, this brilliant bit of conversation would prove your point. Every member of your audience has had a part in such give-and-take conversation. For that reason, they would get your point. So let's agree that any dialogue you write will attempt to get you somewhere. The conversation with the drunk in the bar and grill leads to the gag line. The dialogue with the little redhead in Chap. 12 leads to her explanation of the gadget that sold roasters for her. If in my speech I report that I said "Good morning" to the doorman at the hotel and he said, "Good morning, Mr. Hegarty," I don't seem to be getting any-where. But if I tell you his retort was, "Your fadder's mustache," I am leading you into a struggle. When you write conversation, hit always at the point you want to make.

Such dialogue can be used to break up long stretches of descrip-tion, exposition, or explanation. Let's say this speech of yours is presenting a plan. There are four features to your plan. Under each feature you have listed the reasons why the audience will benefit from that feature. If your first feature had three such reasons, you might write, "The first reason why you'll benefit from this feature is this and this. . . . The second reason is this and this. . . . The third reason is this and this. . . ." Most speakers would handle their reasons why in that manner. But not us. We now know that we could put a little dialogue into one or more of those reasons and make the speech more interesting. We'd write

> The first reason you'll benefit from this feature is this. . . . How do I know? Well, Charlie Whosis says, "This reason is good. I've tried it and it works."

We could carry that conversation with Charlie as far as it served our purpose. We could ask,

"How many times have you tried it, Charlie?"

"Four times yesterday, three times the day before."

"And what happened?"

"Everybody approached but one said 'yes.' "

If it was to your advantage, you could use another question to bring out why that one person said "no." That's always the measure of how far you should go. Will it help you prove a point? If not, you sign off.

It is not difficult to see that such conversation would hold the interest of a group. Of course, you wouldn't have to use it on all your points or all your reasons. But by sprinkling it in with the straight exposition, you get variety that holds interest.

When you use dialogue that comes out of your experience, rewrite it to give it sparkle. Don't use dull conversation. Most small talk is dull. Often you can change a few words and put more life into what you said and he said. Don't worry about trying to make your own speech brilliant. Whenever possible give the smart speech to the other fellow.

When you write dialogue you have to make it sound real. Don't have a mechanic say, "I reinstalled the new engine." He'd probably say, "I put in the new engine." In writing dialogue into your speech you may have to depart from my previous advice about using your own language, for the language of the character in your story may not be yours at all. Don't have your dialogue say, "I'm going to conduct a meeting." Chances are that the man would say, "I'm going to put on a meeting" or "I'm going to run a meeting." Don't write, "I have to prepare an address." Make it "I'm going to write a speech." Certain characters might use that "prepare an address" line. If you are one, use it. But 99.44 per cent of the people you quote will say, "I've got to write a speech."

You can build up any story by conversation. The anecdote in the preceding chapter about the redhead and the gadget that helped her sell roasters could have been built up by adding more dialogue. Here's how.

I had heard about this salesman who had been selling two roasters per day, so when I went into the store I said to the manager, "I hear you got a superman over here who has been selling two roasters per day—can I meet him?"

"You sure can," said the manager, "but it's not a superman, it's a superwoman."

"A woman?" I said.

"Yeah, a woman, a nifty little redhead at that."

You can take it from there. Note, though, that the conversation is natural, the man talks like a store manager. And that's a rule you must follow. If you quote a truck driver, make the words sound like a truck driver, not the English teacher down at the high school. If you quote the English teacher, change the style. Put it in the words of the English teacher, but don't, for goodness' sake, get your wires crossed.

In writing conversation into your speech, don't use such explanations as "he replied" or "he retorted." I mentioned this in Chap. 8, but now we are discussing dialogue and I bring it up again for emphasis. Use only "I asked" and "he said." The other words are used to give variety to a written piece, but from most speakers they sound out of place. To prove this to yourself, try telling a few stories with "he replied" or "he retorted" or similar expressions, then with the simple "ask" and "said." You will sell yourself on using the latter.

Another problem in writing conversation for use in a speech is that you can't use expressions which show how the characters react. You can write: "he said, the color rising to his face," or "his eyes wild with hate." You can't even say, " 'Says who?' he asked sarcastically." It is easy to write such explanations, but you'd sound silly speaking them. If you want to show the feelings of your characters, you have to do it with what they say and the manner in which you report what they say.

A further problem is that the people in your conversation must register their personalities. You have to have a good picture of the people you are quoting and you have to register that picture in the way you report what they say. When you quote Pete, the bar-

tender in the grill across the street, you have to know Pete well
enough to give a good impression of how he would handle the
words of wisdom you are having him say. All characters in your
conversations must have identities. One can talk fast, one slow, one
deep, one high, one Yank, one Southern. Get the idea? For when
you do this conversation, it must sound real.

You can get such gossip for your speech by going out and asking
questions of the people you want to quote. Ask questions, listen to
their answers, and then write the questions and the answers into
your speech.

You know the point you want to illustrate. Then ask a question
that will get the kind of answer you want. Perhaps the answer may
not be exactly what you need, but you can revise it to make it fit.
The answer may be too brief—you may understand it, and the man
who makes the statement may understand it—but you want the
audience to understand, so you may have to expand the answer. At
other times, the answer may be too wordy. Then you will have to
get out the blue pencil and cut.

When you are writing your talk, ask questions of the kind of
persons who will be in your audience and you will get answers that
you can use. Then when you do the speech before an audience,
ask questions of the persons who heard you. The answers can be
strengthened and used in later meetings.

No, you don't have to pick gossip out of thin air. You can go out
and manufacture it yourself. Just listen tonight when you ask a
question. One of the audience will say, "I tried that, and this is
what happened." Tomorrow night you can repeat what the fellow
said tonight. Now it's a story, and by quoting your conversation
you have gossip. You make your point, and you drive it home with,
"Last night over in Springfield, so and so said this. . . ."

Conversation can liven your speech. It can help keep the audience awake. Since everybody likes to listen to gossip, they'll invariably start listening again when you tell them this gossip. Therefore,
get some conversation into your talk. What he said to me, what I
said to him—that's the stuff. Write it in. Audiences love to listen
to it.

There have been a lot of suggestions on using conversation in this chapter. Let's review them:

1. Conversation is lively. Description and exposition are dull. Break up the latter with conversation and you have a much livelier speech.
2. Conversation breaks up the body of a speech just as it does a story in a magazine.
3. Audiences listen to conversation, even though it is pointless. They like it, too.
4. Conversation must get you somewhere, if it is to be useful to you. Plan it to help you make your point.
5. When you have a long stretch of straight talk, break it up with conversation.
6. Carry on the conversation as long as it serves its purpose. Don't pad it and don't cut it short.
7. Rewrite all conversation for sparkle. Make it bright and sprightly.
8. Avoid the stiff and stilted. You are better if you don't quote characters who use such language.
9. When the story makes the point so fast that the audience might miss it, build up the story by conversation.
10. Don't use such explanations as "he replied" or "he retorted."
11. Forget the character's reaction as a part of the conversation. Don't use such bits as "he replied, turning red in the face." If you need that reaction, make it a separate sentence, such as "His face got red. I thought he was going to have a stroke."
12. Keep the conversation in character. If a taxi driver is speaking, don't have him use ten-dollar words.
13. Make the personalities register, if possible, in what they say and the way they say it. Try different voices if you can.
14. Build your conversation by research. Ask questions of persons and use their answers to make your speech conversation.

You have stories now, and conversation. Now let's get on to another good interest-holding device—news.

14. Bring in News, but Local News

News will hold interest in your talk, so write some in. You say your subject is as old as the hills, that there is nothing new about it. Are you sure? Perhaps the news is not on the surface for everybody to see. Let's have a look at what we mean by news.

There are a number of classifications of material that can be used as news in a speech. Here are some of them:

Items from the newspapers or magazines
News angles you develop
A new feature of your product or plan
The unusual—man bites dog stuff
Research you do, or someone else does
A tie-in with today's worries
A hookup with the peeves of the audience
Something you know that the audience does not know

It's not news if water runs under the bridge. However, if the water suddenly turns muddy you have news—a news item that might be put into the speech. Let's say the water running under the bridge started to rise and threatened to wash the bridge downstream. That would no doubt be in the newspaper or on the radio.

The newspaper is a good source of news, perhaps the best. If your subject is live enough to be in today's newspapers, or to tie in with an item in today's newspapers, you are lucky. You might take a clipping from this morning's newspaper out of your pocket. You might spill an envelope full of clippings on the table in front of you. Wouldn't that help make your point?

It is not too difficult to get news angles out of the newspaper. Here are a number of headlines that came out of last night's paper:

RUSSIANS' PRESENCE RETARDING RECOVERY

MANN TELLS NEW STORY OF FAUST

HINTS NEW ATOM ARMS

NEW ORGAN TO BE DEDICATED SUNDAY

VETERANS TOP RENTAL LISTS

BUSINESSES INSTALL COIN-CHANGING DEVICES

TWA CUTS FLIGHT FARE

NEW MOVIE PROJECTOR AT SCHOOL

SEEK MISSING MAIL POUCH AND $80,000

Each of those headlines could be used in a speech. Surely if you wanted to tie your subject up to the news of the day, one of those items would serve, no matter what your subject. Let's say you were planning to talk on "The Efficiency of the Worker." Not one of those headlines is on that subject. Not one seems even close. But let's see what we can do with them.

Take the first one—surely the Russians are efficient. You could talk about the efficiency of the Communist party worker. He is efficient at tearing down. You are talking about efficiency at building up. If you were trying to prove that workers should be more efficient, you could cite the efficiency of the Communist party worker as what our workers should have. You want a like zeal, a similar persistence, a dedication to a cause.

The second headline, MANN TELLS NEW STORY OF FAUST, has to do with a list of new books for the city library. Efficiency—what is more efficient than the city library? You don't like that? Then talk about the efficiency of distribution of books in this country.

That third headline, HINTS NEW ATOM ARMS. Remember the secrecy of the work on the original atom bomb? There is an example of efficiency, of what can be done when all work together. Can't you see the possibilities?

NEW ORGAN TO BE DEDICATED SUNDAY. That next headline does not seem to offer much. It was a story about a small church that had bought a new organ, and this Sunday there was to be a service dedicating the organ. Nothing much on efficiency. Who said so? It was a small church and the money for that organ was raised in a short time. How about the efficiency with which the campaign to raise the funds was organized and run? There is your tie-in.

VETERANS TOP RENTAL LISTS. This one offers more of a problem. Here is what the article said:

> Veterans and their families must be offered the first chance at renting new houses or apartments, or offered the first chance to buy new houses for sale, according to Joe Whosis, Federal rent director of this area.
>
> The law, known as the "Veterans Preference Provision of the Housing and Rent Act of 1948," provides for fines up to $5000 or a prison sentence of not more than one year, or both, for violation of any part of the law.

That doesn't give you much to go on, does it? But there must be an efficiency tie-in somewhere. How about in the job the veterans' organizations did to get the provision written in the bill? Perhaps that is it.

The next seems easy—BUSINESSES INSTALL COIN-CHANGING DEVICES. Here is a machine that replaces workers, in a rather difficult job, too. Your point can be made on the inefficiency of workers that made the installation necessary, or on the efficiency of the machine.

You would not have too much trouble with the next one—TWA CUTS FLIGHT FARE. This had to do with the reduction by 5 per cent of round-trip fares on certain flights. That could be due to the improved efficiency of the operation of the line. It is seldom that a carrier reduces fares without a reduction in costs. The article made some other points too. It said that the company was the largest in the world in terms of miles flown. There could be an efficiency tie-in in that fact.

NEW MOVIE PROJECTOR AT SCHOOL. Our next headline gives us an opportunity to talk about the efficiency or inefficiency of our educational system. Here is proof that the school is using visual education, teaching youngsters through the movies, which the kids like. Surely schools have been using movies for a long time, but this is a grade school and the machine was brought by the PTA. Perhaps a tie-in with the PTA might be suggested. But efficiency can be tied in in any number of ways.

The last headline—SEEK MISSING MAIL POUCH AND $80,000—was the start of a story that told that a mail pouch with $80,000 in it disappeared between Waukesha, Wisconsin, and Chicago, Illinois. Here you can tie in with the efficiency of the post-office department in handling such shipments, or of the post-office depredations unit in checking on such losses, or of the FBI in following the thief. There are two suggestions. You may think of more.

The other headline on the page was HOROSCOPE. That is good for an angle any day. It is always there and perhaps 95 per cent of your audience knows nothing about astrology. Let's say you tell the persons in the room:

"The astrological forecast for this day stresses a very exceptional and fertile state of mind and emotions."

That is what the newspaper said. It would be a good lead for a talk that tried to get the by-laws changed or the dues raised, wouldn't it?

Those headlines were not taken from page 1. They were on an inner page of a small-town newspaper on a Saturday night, when the paper is light. Yet every one of them can be used. I realize that it took some stretching of the imagination to make some of them work, but I did that to show you how. News is interesting to audiences. If your subject is live enough to have a tie-in with today's newspaper, it is worth listening to.

If your subject is not in the newspapers, your next best bet is to manufacture some news about it. Let's say you go out to that bridge mentioned earlier in this chapter. You take a stick and stir up the water. Something happens and you report that something in your speech. That's the kind of news the picture magazines make. They do not have enough news pictures to fill up the magazine, so they take a series of pictures and write a story about something that is not news and might not be rated as news unless they made a story on it.

Here's an example. I tell the group that the users who buy our product like it. Then I say I am going to tell them why I know these users like it. I describe a mail survey I have made. I tell about the postcards that have come back. I read a few of the postcards. I make my point by manufacturing some news about the product and the point.

Much speech material comes out of this sort of activity. The speaker uses surveys that magazines make, that organizations finance. He quotes Gallup polls and Hooper ratings. The news he gives out is manufactured news. Last night I heard a speaker tell about conditions all over the world. He had visited the countries and he had gathered his material. The audience listened with interest because he was comparing what we had with what those other countries had.

In this case the speaker had knowledge that we did not have. For that reason it was news to us. That goes for a lot of things you know that the audience does not know. The fact that you have five boys, or that your wife is left-handed, or that you drive a Plymouth, or work in an air-conditioned office. The audience can't know those things and when you use them in your speech you are serving up news.

When you use this sort of material you are making news, manufacturing it through research. You have dug into history, you have produced some facts and figures. This is what you find. Since the audience didn't dig and get your findings, what you tell them is news to them.

News is something the other fellow doesn't know. Tell him a fact he doesn't know and you may add interest to your talk. It always pays to dig up a few such facts about your subject. And don't reject the old. Even that may have some news angle. The subject you're talking about may be quite old, but somebody said something about it yesterday or somebody did something with it today. Tell about what that somebody did or said and you have news.

The unusual—the unusual reason for giving to the fund, for join-
ing the club, or the unusual use of an old product—makes news too.
Let's say your talk is about an electric washing machine that has
been on the market for years and years. It is the same machine, no
new features, no news value. Well, why not check around to find
an unusual application of that washer. Let's say you find a bank
using it to wash dirty one-dollar bills. That would be a break,
wouldn't it?

In your talk you describe how they do it. Can't you see how you
can bring every operation feature of the washer into such a description? You have an old subject, but you have found an unusual angle
that helps make the old story more interesting.

There is news value in the day's worries. Always those who
worry are looking for something to worry about. That's why the
"view-with-alarm" angle is used in so many speeches. Is there anything in your subject that lends itself to such a tie-in? Can you
produce something that will give worriers something new to worry
about? The worrier who has ten items to worry about now will
love you for giving him number eleven.

There are many things to worry about if you are so minded.
Business, profits, your salary, your taxes, business controls, government spending, foreign policy, the Democrats, the Republicans,
the price of wheat, meat, butter, the high cost of living, the attitude
of the young, the attitude of the old, the liberals, the conservatives.
Yes, out of that list you can find something to tie in with your
speech.

If the talk is to be given to the boys from the club, what is their
pet peeve? Bring it out in the open, mention it, talk about it seri-
ously or kid about it, but don't, for goodness' sake, ignore it.

The peeves of any audience are good talk material. A speaker
tells you how his wife insists on lighting the dinner table with
candles. Most men in the audience go through the same ordeal
whenever they have company. With a wonderful invention like
the electric light, women insist on eating by candlelight. Now that
is good speech material. I have heard it used. Lipstick on water-

cooler bubblers is another good peeve that gets the men. Ah, yes, there are lots of them.

But don't talk about last month's peeve. This is a changing world. The thing that is in the public's mind today is gone tomorrow. Once a man could say "twenty-three, skiddoo" in his talk and prove that he was up-to-date. But you've got to use today's "twenty-three, skiddoo" to prove that you are a ball of fire. I can't write what that is today because by the time this book sees print—even though it be but thirty days from now—the expression may be dead. Just look how long a story holds the front page of a newspaper. Today the editors give you details and tomorrow they throw away the story completely or put it on a back page.

A bit of today in your speech shows the audience that you have some blood in your veins, that you are alive and kicking. Use a phrase from a song that the public is singing—number one on the Hit Parade—or that slang expression that everyone is using. Talk about some argument that you got into on a subject that's hot today. Show that you are awake, that you observe things, that you know the score.

Don't be afraid to use the popular radio gag or to mention the radio program. Let them know that you listen to the radio—and not only to the symphonies. Perhaps you don't like popular music or the present fad in crooners. But don't be afraid to let on that there are such things. Let the audience know that you know what is going on in this old world of ours. Don't concentrate on the good old days. Talk about today. That is what news is.

When you go out to lunch what do you talk about? Business, yes, but what else? Well, it's what's in the newspapers, or in *Time*, or *Newsweek*, or on the radio or television. And it's baseball or football or hockey or basketball or golf. All of these subjects are alive. They are what makes for interesting small talk. And they make good speech material too.

But in using this material bring it home to me. Get it as close to my town, to Seventh and Main, as you can. If you can get it closer to the chair I'm sitting in, you'll interest me. Once when I was doing a series of talks about air conditioning I found that no one seemed to appreciate the value of fresh air or moving air. No one seemed to realize what a lack of fresh, moving air meant. They lived in rooms for years without adequate fresh air and no one ever told them that the air they were breathing wasn't fit to breathe. There was news of the highest value.

In this talk, I used the story of the Black Hole of Calcutta, of the people imprisoned in the small room who died because they couldn't get fresh air and air movement. Still the audience didn't appreciate what I was talking about.

Then I started talking about the air in the room the audience was in. That was their air. It was the air they were breathing. I described the conditions in the room, I pointed out the little holes through which air came into the room, the small crack in the windows which were open. I talked about the smoke with which they filled the room. On top of that I pictured each of them breathing in and breathing out that same air over and over again. I called it "secondhand air." As I went on talking I could see them beginning to perspire, beginning to feel uncomfortable. Men stirred in their chairs, others got out handkerchiefs and mopped their brows. By bringing my example into the room and to the chairs in which they were sitting, my news of fresh air meant something to them. Before I called their attention to the conditions, the air in the room was all right. Now they found it uncomfortable. The absence of fresh air was news to them.

Perhaps you won't have anything so close to your audience as the air they are breathing. But it illustrates my point. If you can get your story in terms of the air they are breathing, the temperature of the room, the hard chairs they are sitting on, then you have something that certainly will hold their interest.

With experience you can find news in any subject. Perhaps you are covering the same subject, the same plan, the same product. Okay, why not look for a news angle?

Look for a new use, some new concept, some engineering or psychological approach. You may find any one of them. If not, think back to this morning's newspaper. What item did you find that struck you as interesting? That item probably hit the audience too. Here's what I mean. Not so long ago a couple was married by a minister in California. Now there is no news in that because couples are being married by ministers in California every day. But in this case the minister was a baby four years old. Going up in the office elevator one morning someone mentioned it. That noon at lunch someone brought it into the conversation. Later, in the barbershop, the boss quoted the priest who said that the youngster was no more capable of witnessing the contract than Charlie McCarthy. That shows why, when you mention an item in the morning's newspaper, members of the audience nod their heads. They read about it too, and you are adding interest and demanding attention when you use such items. Such news is all around you. Keep your eyes and ears open and use what you find.

Well, if that's true, you ask, why don't more speakers use such items? I can't answer that question. It's probably because they don't know that such items help make their talk more interesting.

So let's write some news into your speech. Not last week's news. Today's news. That is what this audience will go for.

Now let's get on to the next idea, which has to do with the makers of news—people.

15. Talk about People

People are most interested in people—news about people, gossip about names, conversations about individuals. When you write your speech, put in something about the individuals in the room, about the family, about the men who work at the office, about the neighbors.

You don't need any proof of our interest in individuals. Just look at the morning newspaper. I did that this morning. Here are the headlines in the first ten stories: MAN JAILED IN MEETING WILL TESTIFY; BIKE SHOWER SPICES GIRL'S FIFTH BIRTHDAY; ATTACK VICTIM GOES HOME; GOVERNOR TO GIVE OUT TRUE WORD; BOAT SINKS— OVER TWENTY DIE; CITY CHIEF TELLS OF THREATS; ECA SPOKESMAN SAYS.

Get the idea? Today's newspaper is no different from tomorrow's. Almost every story in that newspaper has people in it. When you release a publicity story about a talk you're going to give, you have to put the names of some persons in it. A headline like "Ajax Company Declares Dividends" will be followed by a headline which tells what the president of Ajax says. In other words, some person is in it. Persons make news and the mention of persons makes for interest in your speech.

Now who are these people who make good speech material? Almost everybody, but let's list a few of them.

The men in the meeting room, the chairman, the man who arranged for your appearance, the members of the club that you know.

Then there is the family—the wife and kids, the brother-in-law, the relatives. Look how Bob Burns, the comedian, has made a living talking about his kin. You can talk about yours and the audience will be interested.

Another group is the neighbors. All of your audience have neighbors who borrow from them, who watch them, whose dogs get into their gardens, who complain when their dogs get on the wrong side of the fence. Yes, neighbors are good material.

Then there are your business associates, your boss, his boss, the men in your share-the-ride club, the receptionist, the office boy, the stenographer.

Add next the people everybody knows, the taxi drivers, the tough cops, the bus drivers, your fellow commuters, the butcher, baker, candlestick maker—this is a large group.

Then come the names, the big names of today and the big names of history. Today's are best, but the ones out of the past are good too.

That's quite a group of possibilities, isn't it? That first group, the members of the club, are a big help in getting started. Always when I start a speech, I say something about the chairman. I speak about "old Russ" as if he and I were bosom pals of long standing. Perhaps I have just met him for the first time, but I talked to him at the cocktail party or during the dinner and I have learned something about his business or his golf game, or his boxer dogs. So when I start off, I mention this bit of information I gleaned. Russ loves that and so does the club. I try, too, to bring in the man who arranged for my appearance, or an acquaintance I ran into. Such talk interests the club members. It also stamps you as one of them. I have a regular routine in which I quote what various members have said to me. The club eats it up. Perhaps you have noticed how the hired entertainer always mentions the man who hires him. Follow this plan; it is good business.

Then don't neglect your family. Bring in the wife and kids. They are excellent speech material. Most men writing a speech to be given in public hesitate to write in the family. They feel a little embarrassed. But they are wrong on that. The family—the wife, the kids, the dogs and cats—are possessions that stamp you as the same kind of person as those in this audience. They have kids, they have a wife, they have dogs, some of them have cats. The problems at your home, which you think are peculiar to you, are also their problems.

Tell how the Missus plays bridge even though she has taken all those lessons. Explain how your sister-in-law won't let her husband sit in the white chair. Then talk about the mean aunt who won't allow any dogs in the house. Your boy of high-school age and his high opinion of you always brings a smile to the faces of the listeners. They have kids with similar lofty opinions.

Write into this speech what the wife said about your good judgment if it helps you prove a point. Tell a story about what your kids did in a certain situation if that helps prove a point. Don't bring in the wife and kids just for the fun of bringing them in or to let the audience know that you have them. Use them and anecdotes about them and gossip with them to help put over your points.

One such story I've told over and over in a number of talks has to do with my number one son. Here's the story:

> We had just finished dinner and were sitting around talking when this youngster said, "Well, I have to go up now and work on my trigonometry for three hours."
>
> I asked him, "Why don't you keep up-to-date in your homework?"
>
> "I do," the youngster said. "This is just today's work."
>
> "What do you mean?" I asked. "You mean to say that they give you three hours' homework to do in one night?"
>
> "Yes, they do," he said.
>
> "That's ridiculous, no teacher would do a thing like that. How many problems do you have?"
>
> "Well," he said, "I have twelve problems."
>
> "I can do them in thirty minutes," I said.
>
> Well, those rash words resulted in a dollar bet that I couldn't. So off he went upstairs to get his trigonometry book, his notebook, and a pencil. When he came back he threw the whole in front of me and said, "There you are. You do them while I time you."
>
> "No, that's not the way we're going to do it," I said. "Here, you take the book, the pad, and the pencil."

He took them. I asked him to read the first problem. When he had finished, I asked, "What is the cosine?"

He replied, "It's this side of the triangle over this side."

Then I asked another question, "What is the cotangent?" for that was the other factor in this problem. Again he explained what it was and then he added, "Okay, I can work this one." He made a few figures on the page and looked in the back of the book and seemed surprised. In less than a minute he had the correct answer. I suggested that he look at the clock.

"We took fifty seconds on that one," I said.

"You're lucky," he growled.

Then I had him read the second problem, with the same result. On the third the procedure was about the same.

We worked the first three problems in two minutes and fifty seconds. Then he picked up his book, his pad of paper, and his pencil and went on up to his room. "I can work the rest of them," he told me. As he passed his mother in the living room he said, "That old bird sure knows his trig."

I've used that story to demonstrate the value of asking questions in determining what the prospect wanted to buy. I've used it to illustrate the value of method. The boy knew what the different terms in trigonometry meant. I didn't know that at all. But I did have one knowledge that he didn't have. I knew method. I knew how to solve a problem by asking questions about it.

That illustrates how you can use stories about the family and about the kids. And when I've done this talk in speeches it has held interest because the listeners have families, too, and they will listen with interest when I talk about mine.

Talk about the neighbors. That's another thing that everybody has. Talk about your share-the-ride club. The neighbor who sweeps off the walk every morning. The blonde next door who wears slacks. Everybody has such neighbors and when you talk about them you will hold interest. Time and again a member of an audience has told me, "I have a neighbor just like that."

Write into your talk the kind of people everybody knows. The hotel clerks, bus drivers, bartenders, janitors, maids, grocers, butchers. But don't talk about taxi drivers all the time. Now a taxi driver, now a bartender, now the hotel clerk. All these people can add interest to your speech.

In mentioning persons always use their names. Don't say, "I was talking to a fellow in a nearby town." Name the fellow and name the town. Many speakers hesitate to mention friends by name. That's wrong. If a story about one of the group will help make a point, use the story and name the man. The audience likes to hear about its friends. If you establish yourself as a friend of one of their friends, you are close to a friend of the group.

The other night I spoke to a Cooperative Club. The president, who sat next to me at dinner, had a list of the membership before him. I read through the list and noted that a number of my friends were not present that night. When I started to speak I called off the names of those friends who hadn't appeared. I told the club that these people were friends of mine, real friends. And since they knew the kind of speaker I was, they stayed home. That made a big hit with the audience. The men mentioned were my friends and their friends, and I was using sure-fire material when I mentioned them.

When you mention names you can be certain you have with you the people whose names you mention. Everybody is glad to be mentioned. The other day I told a friend, "I mentioned your name in my speech."

"You mentioned it twice," he corrected.

Yes, they love it. Tell what the chairman said and he loves it. But don't wait until you get to the head table to think of this. No, write that fellow in while you're getting your talk on paper. If you want to quote the chairman on a subject, ask him a question about that subject, then use his answer. Many times when you say that Bill Whosis did something or said something, a voice from the audience will respond, "He would." Well, you're cooking with electricity when they nib in.

Many speakers go in for big names. They quote Abraham Lincoln or Oliver Cromwell. Perhaps that helps. My thought is that any quotation you attribute to a big name would be stronger if you said that someone they knew said it. Let's say you quoted the big shot. Where are you then? You haven't said anything and there is little news in what these big shots say. Particularly if Mr. Big has been dead for a hundred years. But if Joe Blow said it, there's a difference. Joe is a friend, a pal. What's good enough for Joe is good enough for them. There is little preaching in what Joe says. There is none of the stuffed shirt. For that reason Joe's cracks have a much better chance of going over.

I once had a friend who seldom made a speech without some such reference as "I think it was Cato who said—." Then he quoted Cato. Well, we all figured he read that out of a book some place. We felt that it hadn't come out of his experience. Perhaps reading a book is experience, but it didn't seem that way to us. Now if he had said, "The bartender down at the Elite said," we would have been all ears because we know Pete and we know that Pete is a character who gets off some pretty good cracks.

The other night I heard a speaker tell about his conversations with all the political leaders of Europe. He had been in twenty or more countries and had met and talked to the leaders. As he quoted what these men told him, it was just as if you or I were quoting the driver on the Seventh Street bus. He knew those men. He was making his points by quoting them. Now that is all right. If you know the big shots, if you are in the habit of talking with them, if you play golf with them, fine, go on and quote them. Perhaps you are a big shot yourself. Then what the president said to you, or the vice-president, or the senator may be okay. If you bring it in, bring it in quite naturally. But when you're a little guy and attempt to bring in the big shots of a bygone era, you seem to get yourself out of character. You'll do much better if you stick to the boys of this day and age. Perhaps Oliver Cromwell did say, "When you stop getting better you stop being good." But Pete, the bartender, might say that too. And it sounds more natural if you quote Pete rather than the departed Oliver.

You can suit yourself on this point. Some instructors of public speaking advise you to quote Cato and Oliver Cromwell. In my suggestions on how to write a unit, I call for such quotations. But I am not comfortable quoting these big names out of the past. I always wonder whether or not the man quoted really said what I say he said. I feel, too, as if I am trying to parade a knowledge that I do not have. I have used all of them, the ancients, the poets, the men who run the club before which I am speaking, the ordinary characters that are in my life, the wife and kids. God bless them all! They have made excellent speech material for me. They will do the same for you. So write them in, these nice people. Remember that the number one interest of any audience is— people. And, of course, his favorite of all people is he—himself.

Let's run over again the kind of people that make for interesting material in a speech.

1. The persons in the meeting, the chairman, the members and the guests.
2. The family—the wife and kids, the girl friend, the in-laws, the relatives. What they do, say, or think is interesting.
3. The neighbors, their kids, their dogs, their gardens.
4. The associates at the office. The boss and his screwy ideas. The fellow in the next office and his pipe.
5. The big names, the names that everyone knows.
6. The little people of the world that everybody knows. The redcaps, the bellhops, the newsboys.

Talk to people, all kinds of people. Listen to them. Then write descriptions of their actions into your speeches. If the audience is interested in people, cater to that interest.

16. Don't Slight Your Possessions

Just like people, your possessions come high on the list of interest builders in a speech. Bring them in, mention them—your cat, your dog, your car, your Sunday suit. Common experiences, the trouble you had getting your suit pressed, or the way the coins spilled when you tried to rob the kid's piggy bank.

The suit that you are wearing, the pants that show the shine, the hat that cries aloud for cleaning—all such things can be brought into the speech in a way that will create interest in the audience. For these are the things those people out front know. One man's hat needs cleaning, another's shoes need new heels. When you talk about these things, you are one of them. And when you show that you are the kind of Joe that has the same problems, you're talking right down their alley.

I use a lot of this sort of material in my speeches. I use my clothes, the things around the house, my projects, the painting of the bathroom, the flower garden by the garage, the things in my office, my desk, my chair, the ceiling that the workmen seem to step through so often, the lighting, the poor ventilation, my car and its peculiarities. All these are speech material, material that seems to interest audiences when I use it in my speeches.

How do you use such possessions? Well, let's take clothes as an example. Once in a series of meetings I wore a red necktie. At the first meeting, as I was introduced, a man in the audience called, "Ah, a guy with a red necktie!"

Well, salesmen wear neckties. Through a break, I had an opportunity to build something out of that tie. Here is the way I handled it. I said, "Yes, a red necktie." Then I pulled the tie out of my vest so that they could see the whole dollar-and-a-half worth of red. Then I went on, "When they asked me to talk to this group they told me that you were a red-hot sales force. So I put on the hottest tie I have—I wore it to remind me to be good."

To show how important the right attitude is, a friend of mine, Cy Burg, vice-president of the Iron Fireman Company and one of the best speakers I know, illustrates a point with a story about a gray suit of clothes, a white shirt, and a red tie. Thus:

> There are lots of ways to express enthusiasm. I want to give you one quickly. I got my clue one gloomy Monday morning from a sorry-looking salesman who got into my office. He was dressed in a black suit, black socks, black briefcase, black tie, black overcoat, and black hat. How he got in, I don't know. There he came, slouching into the office with that run-down expression. I could see that he hadn't sold anything in six weeks.
>
> He said, "Good morning, Mr. Burg. How's business?" Remember in those days how you used to ask people how business was— "Hello, Sam, how is business?"
>
> That was the day when pessimism was everywhere.
>
> Well, this fellow said to me, "How is business?"
>
> I said, "Fine."
>
> "Fine?" He looked at me closely. His mouth dropped open.
>
> I said, "Yes, it's fine. We're running 30 per cent ahead of last year."
>
> He said, "You're the first man in six months that told me that business was good. You don't want to buy a new automobile, do you?"
>
> I thought, "My God, no, not from that gloom peddler."
>
> But that peddler of gloom gave me an idea. Here it is—
>
> How much better would it have been if he had come in dressed up in—well, a light gray suit, why not? A gray suit is more cheerful than a black one. It doesn't have to be summer to wear gray, and the gray hat that goes with it. And why not a white shirt and a red tie—the red tie is much more cheerful than black. Here I'll show you. (The speaker takes off his blue tie and puts on a red one.) Don't I look more cheerful now and more optimistic?
>
> The silly part is that it works. I made this talk at a Rotary Club

in Cleveland. Next morning a friend called me and said, "Cy, it works."

"Who's this? What works?" I asked.

"This is Bill—the gray-suit-and-red-tie idea. It's terrific; the thing worked. You know what I did this morning? Although it's snowing, I got out one of last summer's gray suits and a red tie and went down to the office. I've been working on a prospect for nine months. The guy has been saying "no" for nine months, and I said to myself, "This guy is going to say 'yes' this morning." I tried this theory of yours and I have just come back with the biggest order in my life. Thanks, Cy, for the tip."

Now it wasn't the tie, it wasn't the suit. The change was made in his head. It was a change in his mental attitude. Mental attitude is everything. If you can just train salesmen to have the right mental attitude, they will go to town and they will sell. They might not have the right approach, they might stumble through the presentation, but if they have the right attitude and see enough people, they will sell.

The heroes in that story are a gray suit and a red necktie. And you should listen while Cy Burg tells the story. If you heard him do it once, you would realize how powerful an argument you can make with such items of clothing. Perhaps it is because the men in that audience all have gray suits and red ties. When you speak of such things they understand and sympathize.

You might have a much more interesting story about the moon, the planets, or the stars, but the men and women in the audience don't own such celestial bodies. Thus when you illustrate a point by telling them your experience in trying to get your old hat cleaned, they ride right along with you. They have had that kind of experience, too.

I have a story I use about a button on my overcoat. Last year when I was going to make a talk out of town, I lost a button off my overcoat. I heard it drop between the back door and the garage. I stopped to hunt for it. I moved the car. I couldn't find it. So I was forced to go on the trip without the button.

In the first town on the trip I tried to buy a button. I went into a number of stores. I looked for the notion counters. I had always felt that old ladies run notion counters. But I found only kids behind the counters, and those kids had no interest in a fat man who had lost a button off his overcoat.

Now that's good speech material. Any member of the audience can imagine the same thing happening to him. So I made a story out of losing the button off my overcoat, my search for a button to replace it, and a needle and thread to sew it on. I used it to show how little interest salespeople have in serving customers today.

The illustration worked well for me. It was so close to the experiences of others that everybody in the room could picture my experiences.

Your pets also make excellent speech material. I've used the rabbits who eat the young plants that come up in the spring. I've used Judy, a neighbor's dog that comes to our back door begging for food. I don't know who owns her. She looks hungry but she's fat. And all the neighbors feed her. I don't feed her because I wouldn't want a dog of mine fed away from home. Still, she doesn't stop asking. Somehow it seems that dog is psychic. Whenever we're having roast beef at our house, she is at our back door waiting for a handout. That dog is good for a number of stories that make good speech material. She has been used time and again to prove that it pays to ask for the order.

Your home makes excellent speech material. I am one of these fellows that tinker, and the story of the leak in the roof I tried to fix and how I didn't quite do it has been used to make the point that when you have a job that needs an expert, it is best to call in an expert. On the other hand, I fixed the crack in the plaster that the wallpaper hangers couldn't. That made speech material to prove that fools rush in where angels fear to tread. The fingermarks that the kids leave on the back door have been used too. The marks get my goat. The kids don't see them. I prove that by asking them with some authority to take a damp rag and wipe off the marks. But next day the marks are back. I use that to make the point that it is useless to worry about small things. The leaky faucets that the Missus is after me to fix—those, too, are good. She doesn't want me to tinker with the utilities, but she keeps after me to fix those faucets. I use that to prove the uncertainties of life or the inconsistency of women. All of it goes through the mill and comes out point-making speech material.

Then there are my projects. My garden took an awful beating when, during the war, we were growing for victory. The robins wanted the strings that marked my seed rows. Every morning they would try to fly off with those strings. A bird would take the string in its beak and start to fly off, but the strings were anchored and the bird would get about six feet and would be stopped short. It would tumble in the air. But it would not stop. Back it would go and try the same thing all over again. I used the story of those birds to show that persistence pays. Eventually they got the strings.

The Scout troop made a lot of such stories—how the kids felt about the grownups, how I got the fathers to come to the meetings. Stories on these activities helped me make points. My club is another good provider of speech material. Here I tell how they stick me with the various jobs, how the brass in the club think they are sticking me but how I really like it. That goes over well with club audiences. I always use such stories to make the point that the member who works gets more out of the club. No club member who works for his club is going to hate me for that.

Your church is another good source of speech material. Every one of the audience feels that he should go to church. It helps you with them if you admit that you do. I tell them that I always sit in the front pew on Sunday. I do that with the hope that others will follow my lead, for if they do, the priest or minister will have the seats close to him filled. I tell this story to make the point that if the audience is close to the speaker, the speaker will be better. He will get the feel of the group, he will feel a response that he could never get if he were talking to two or three rows of empty seats. Empty seats are cold and unfriendly; seats filled with people are warm and friendly.

Then there is your office. For years I have been trying to get the fellows who run the air conditioning to get some air into my office. I am not interested in cooling; all I want is fresh air. Well, the mechanics came and went, they adjusted everything, but nothing happened. I still got no fresh air. Then this winter someone discovered that the air duct running into my office had been dead-ended before it reached my office. That was grand. They fixed the duct and I began to get the much-needed air. But in working above the ceiling one of the workmen stepped through the plaster in two places. So for a month I had two holes in my office ceiling. I can use that story to show that a man should be satisfied with his lot. Stories can be slanted to make points out of all the things in the office—the pen and pencil set, the creak in my chair, the bookcase, the campaign I run to keep things off the file cabinet, and how everybody seems to be intent on cluttering up the place. That is all good speech material, for every man with an office has some of it.

I do a number of talks on selling and use a number of stories about trying to get adjustments on things I have bought. Not long ago we broke the top of our glass coffeemaker. Well, I went to every store in town that carried that kind of coffeemaker and none of them had a spare top. None of them knew when they might have one and, further, none of them seemed to worry too much about whether or not they would ever have one. About that time up in Cleveland I spent a whole afternoon looking for one of those tops. The reception in the stores was much the same as I had received in the stores at home. I wrote a letter to the manufacturer. I got a nice reply stating that I should go to a store and buy one.

My letter had told about my attempts to buy one in nine stores, but apparently the manufacturer did not read that part. Well, I saw the name of the president of the company in a trade paper, and I wrote a letter to him and marked the letter "personal." I told about my search and asked him to send me a top C.O.D. In about ten days I got a letter from the service manager. He told me that he was sending me a top free of charge but that his action was not to be taken as a precedent, that my coffeemaker was out of the guarantee period, and next time I broke a top I was to buy one from a dealer and pay for it. Now there is material on which any speaker can go to town. It proves that some companies are mishandling customers. It shows that it is the little things that make friends for companies. It proves that when you buy a product that does not work, you can get quick action by writing the president. Every day something happens to you and your possessions that will make such speech material.

Your car is a fine topic for speeches. Almost everyone in the audience has a car and has had similar experiences. I use one story about trying to get the mechanics at the service station to put another thermostat in my car. I tried and tried, but they wouldn't do it. I couldn't figure why, unless they felt that by doing it they would prove I was right in my diagnosis of what was wrong. Then one day when I had the car out of town I drove into a service station, asked to have a new thermostat put in, and stood for perhaps fifteen minutes while the job was done. After that I had no more trouble. Then one day back at my own service station the mechanic said, "Don't have any more trouble with that thermostat, do you, Mr. Hegarty?" I told him I didn't. "I knew it wasn't that," he said.

With that story I make the point that a salesman should allow the customer to talk. Sometimes the customer might have a good idea.

Even a small thing like a nail clip can be made into a story. I tell about the time I went into a drugstore to buy a nail clip. I told the clerk what I wanted. He went into the back and came out with one. He laid it on the counter. I picked it up and asked, "How much?"

"Twenty-five cents," he said, "and it's pretty good too."

I use that to show that a salesman should say something positive about his wares. He should have said, "It's made of good steel" or "It's got a fine cutting edge." His "pretty good too," added nothing and would have been better left unsaid. So I use that story as one of my examples of why a salesman should accentuate the positive.

Don't be afraid to get personal in talking about your possessions. If you wear a toupee, talk about that. Did you ever hear a fellow who wore a toupee mention it? Not so you can notice it. But wouldn't such a mention keep the audience awake?

If you have a joke to tell, always make the joke pretty much on you. Don't make yourself the butt of jokes, but let them know that there have been times when you weren't too smart. Tell these anecdotes about the things you own in a way that gives the audience the pleasure of anticipating what's going to happen. If they know what is going to happen, they will enjoy the story much better. Then at the end you might fool them by having something different happen.

That's enough of examples. Remember that the mention of possessions will add the little touches that help make your talk interesting. So write them in. The more visionary your subject, the more you should try to bring in some of the ordinary, everyday, humdrum activities. The possessions mentioned here are that kind of material. They help add color to your story, help stamp you as the same type of fellow that makes up your audience.

Let's review the possessions that can make good speech material:

1. Your clothes—the ones you wear, the ones you would like to wear, the ones you buy for the kids.
2. Your pets—your dog, your cat, your horse. Think how many dollars radio sponsors have paid to comedians for mentioning Bing Crosby's race horses.
3. Your home—the lawn, the roof, the screen door, the storm windows, the view into the neighbor's garage.
4. Your projects—your garden, your bridge club, your basement workshop—there are millions of them.
5. Your office—the desk, the table, the bookcase, the chair, the battle to get carpet on the floor.

6. Your purchases—all of your adventures with tradesmen go well. All can be used to prove points.
7. Your car—the old stand-by, your battle to make it run, to make it stop.

These are but a few. You take it from here. But use these possessions of yours to prove a point or two.

17. Dramatize Some Points

One of the best means of holding interest as you talk is to dramatize some points. The audience will get tired of talk, talk, talk. So you must do something—wave your arms, shout, do a little dance, show them something, demonstrate a device. All these and anything like them, for the purpose of this discussion, I call "dramatizations."

Even the simplest gesture makes a talk more interesting. So let's plan some of these gestures. If you are equal to it, let's plan some demonstrations. If you can bring yourself to do it, perhaps some horseplay, a stunt or two. Now don't say, "I can't do anything like that." If you can't, you are most unusual. I've taught the most diffident and reserved fellows to do stunts before audiences they would never have thought of doing. True, the men had to force themselves to do the stunts, but they did them well and added interest to their talks.

In Chap. 16 I told about a speaker who changed his tie before an audience. Now most speakers would never attempt to do a thing like that. They would be embarrassed. They may have seen other speakers do it, but their reaction has been, "Well, he's the kind of a fellow that could do that. I'm not."

I have had men say that to me. I always ask, "Why can't you do that?"

"Well, a man has to be a certain type to do a stunt like that—pretty much of an extrovert, I'd say."

"You mean he has to be a little nuts?" I asked.

"It probably helps."

Well, maybe it does help. But any speaker can do such stunts.

Taking off a tie and putting on another is easy. I have seen a speaker break a skillet with a hammer; I've seen another fall under the table; I have seen one stand on his head. It is true a man has to have a certain amount of skill to stand on his head, but speakers can be taught to handle almost any kind of dramatization.

The speaker who does not ordinarily go in for dramatizations in his talks can start with simple stunts. After that he can go on to more elaborate ones. The point I want to make here is that such stunts should be written into the speech.

If you are going to do any sort of dramatization, you should write out the stage directions. Perhaps you are going to run your hands through your hair, wave your arms, stomp your feet. Write what you plan to do in the script. Put it, "I'll walk two steps to the right. I'll raise my hands above my head and I'll shout." For a lengthy demonstration or dramatization write out all details.

Let's say you are going to show a piece of printed matter. That is a simple act. There are a number of ways you can handle it.

1. You can hold it up and show it.
2. You can take it out of your pocket and show it.
3. You can open the pages one by one and show what is on each.
4. You can write something on it.
5. You can indicate pictures or paragraphs you want the audience to see.

There are, of course, many other things you can do, but these illustrate the point. Any one of these is simple. In a number of cases I have taken a card out of my pocket, held it up for the audience to see, and have said, "The figures on this card are so important that I wrote them out so I would be sure to remember them and give them to you."

One of my friends has a stunt that has helped him a lot. He says that when you are making a speech and have run out of things to say or have forgotten what you meant to say, you take a card out of your pocket. The card may have nothing on it, but you look at the card for a few seconds. If an idea of what you should say comes to you, you go on and express the idea. If your mind still remains a blank after looking at the card, you say, "Well, I guess the other points listed here are not important enough." Saying which you sit down.

In my talk on "How to Run a Sales Meeting" I give an imitation of the speaker who talks from a set of notes written on small cards. Instead of the usual white cards I use a deck of playing cards. I use this stunt to illustrate how speakers fumble with their notes. I say this:

> The biggest fumbler I know is the fellow who does his talk from a set of cards like this. (Show cards.) He stands there with his deck of cards clasped firmly against his fat tummy like this. (Demonstrate.) He goes on making his points. Then he comes to a line, "Gentlemen, the world is going to. . . ."
>
> He stops, for he has lost the idea. So he repeats, "Yes, gentlemen, the world is going to. . . ."
>
> The idea still eludes him and for the third time he says, "Yes, gentlemen, I repeat the world is going to. . . ."
>
> Now he glances surreptitiously at the cards in his hand. A smile lights his face. He looks at the audience and plunges on. "Yes, gentlemen, the world is going to perdition, perdition I say. . . ."
>
> He has seen the Jack of Hearts [show it] and got his cue. Now he takes the Jack and slides it on the bottom. [Do it.]
>
> When you use cards the audience is conscious of them. They watch them and worry. They hope that you have a pinochle deck instead of a full fifty-two-card pack.
>
> All my life, for the thirty-odd years that I have been attending meetings, I have hoped that someday I would see a speaker who shuffled those cards on which he had his notes. You know, gave them this. [Shuffle the cards.]
>
> Well, down in Dayton last year I saw that. The speaker was going along, and since he was nervous, as most speakers are, he started to shuffle his cards. [Shuffle the cards.]
>
> The time came when he needed his next note. He looked at the cards, saw the Ten of Spades [show it] and realized that was not the right card. For a minute he gave it this. [Spread out the cards

and look through them. Act as if you are having trouble with your bifocals.]

After a minute of that, he threw his cards on the table, and from then on his speech was better.

This dramatization adds a lot to that talk of mine. It helps me make the point that card notes are not good. But such a stunt has to be written out and acted out. It is not enough to tell yourself, "When I come to that point I'll do this." No, you had better write stage directions for what you are to do when you reach that point.

The directions should be written, no matter how simple the stunt you are planning. Let's say you plan to run your hand through your hair. All right, which hand—left hand or right hand? Or both hands? Perhaps it would be well to stand in front of the large mirror on the hall-closet door and see how you look running your right hand, or your left hand, or both hands through your hair. You say you know how you look? Listen, you have no idea at all. Perhaps after you see yourself do the stunt in front of a mirror you will decide to forget the whole thing.

Write out directions for that gesture in detail. Where are you planning to stop your hand? Will you lift it off your head or will you run it down to your collar in the back? I am asking because if you are going to write in directions for a gesture, you had better understand just how far you are going to carry the gesture.

Perhaps you have seen Sam Vining, the red-suspender philosopher, run his hands through his hair. You think he is trying to tear his hair out by the roots. But when he reaches his hands up he knows exactly what he is going to do. He doesn't stop one place today and another the next time he does the stunt. No, he does it the same way each time.

That is what I am getting at. A stunt isn't difficult if you have studied what you want to do and know exactly how you are going to do it. Running your hands through your hair is a rela-

tively simple stunt, but even the simple stunts require thought.
And writing out the directions for the stunt makes you do that
thinking.

If you write the directions, you'll think of that demonstration
every time you read over the script in preparation for your
talk.

You'll think of raising your hand, of stomping your feet. What's
more, you'll practice your demonstration just the same as you
practice your talk, and because you do that you'll do the stunt
more effectively when you appear before the audience.

I assume that most of the readers of this book are called upon
to write business talks. They think of such dramatizations in connection with demonstrations of a product or with stunts that help
make points for them. To illustrate what can be done, I'll describe
two such dramatizations that I have used.

One of these illustrated how cooks use too much water in cooking vegetables. We were illustrating the point that with electric
cooking little or no water is necessary. We explained how the
cooks put the vegetables in a pan, covered them with water, and
boiled the water until they thought the vegetables were done.
Then they poured the water down the sink.

Our story was that by using so much water they cooked the
vitamin content of the vegetables into the water, then threw the
water away. This story further explained that it might have been
better to drink the water that was poured down the sink and throw
the overcooked vegetables away.

Now that story is interesting told only in words. But it was
better when the speaker acted as if he held an imaginary pan in
one hand and held the lid on top of the pan with the other. He
took a few steps toward an imaginary sink and gave a demonstration of a cook pouring water off the vegetables as he held the lid
in place so that the vegetables would not fall out. Everybody has
seen a cook do this. The demonstration was simple, but it helped
get the point across. Here is how that dramatization was written
into a speech script:

WHAT YOU SAY

WHAT YOU SAY	WHAT YOU DO

Most of us use too much water when we cook vegetables. We put the vegetables—let's say peas—into the pan. Then we fill the pan with water until it covers the peas.

Indicate you are drawing water out of a tap into a pan.

Now we put the pan with the water and peas on the stove. We turn on the heat, and we let the water boil until we think the peas are done. Now, what do we do? That's right, we take a couple of heat pads. With one hand we lift the pan off the stove like this. With the other hand we hold the lid on the pan like this. Now we walk over to the sink and pour the water down the sink.

Act as if you put pan on stove.

Hold hands as if one holds pan, the other holds the lid on top.

Walk to imaginary sink.

What's wrong with that procedure? Simply this—by boiling those peas violently, we boiled most of the vitamin content of those peas into the water. And what did we do with the water? It was poured down the sink. And the vitamins went with it. Why, it would have been more healthful perhaps to drink that water and to throw what was left of the peas down the sink.

Appear to pour water down sink.

Such a dramatization can be carried as far as you want. One day in Cleveland at the Arcade I saw an Indian carrying the pan-and-lid demonstration to its logical conclusion. The Indian was decked out in war paint and all the trimmings. It made little difference that he talked with a Brooklyn accent; he looked like an Indian. To sell his tonic he was using this vitamin story. He told how people cook vegetables in too much water, how they pour the water down the sink. He went through the dramatization by holding his hands as if he had an imaginary pan and lid. He walked over to a sink and poured the water off the vegetables. But did he stop there? No, he did not. He squeezed the last ounce of drama out of his stunt. He added a paragraph to his story that I had not thought of. Here's what he said:

"Well, where do those vitamins go? I'll tell you—they go down into the sewer. And what happens there? The rats eat them and they get strong while you get weak."

That shows how to get the greatest amount of drama out of a demonstration.

I once had a talk to do on the informative label which Westinghouse puts on its appliances. This label is called a "Tell-all Tag." It was quite a remarkable little booklet, for it gave data with which a salesman could answer all the questions that any customer might ask about such products as refrigerators, electric ranges, automatic washers, and other appliances. Now I could have told all those facts. I could have held up a label and shown what was in it. But here's the dramatization I worked out.

I took a set of those labels—the Tell-all Tags that applied to every product—and tied them all together with a red ribbon. There were fifty-three tags and by tying them together I could put them all in my side coat pocket. Here is how such a dramatization is written:

WHAT TO SAY	WHAT TO DO
Gentlemen, in this pocket right here I have all the information a salesman would need to sell any one of the twenty-two Westinghouse appliances. Yes, sir, it's all here, and it's not a big pocket either, is it?	Pull coat pocket around to the front and show it. Make sure that the labels do not bulge too much in the pocket.
Now that sounds remarkable, doesn't it? All the information needed in just one pocket. But it's here. Yes, it's here and I'm going to prove it to you. Watch me now. There it is—fifty-three Tell-all Tags. Yes sir, every one of them, one on every model.	Slap pocket three or four times slowly. Reach hand into pocket and take out the bunch of Tell-all Tags. Spread tags in two hands to show that all the tags are there.
Yes, gentlemen, there it is—all the information that any salesman needs to sell Westinghouse appliances.	Let tags fall in a string. Hold the end high so that the audience can appreciate the number.

In any such dramatization follow these few simple rules:

1. Don't rush it. Take your time. Talk slowly. You want the audience to understand what you are doing.
2. Make sure that the audience can see what you are doing.
3. Plan each movement so that you make everything look easy.
4. Explain what you are doing as you go along.
5. Give reasons why things happen. Say, "I push this button here and this happens. . . ."
6. Hold attention where you want it. Say, "I want you to look at this red lever. . . ."

Check your written stage directions to see that they follow these rules.

If you have not been using such stunts in your speeches, let's try one or two simple ones. Here are a few suggestions:

1. Try one of the more elaborate gestures—raise your hand above your head, or raise both hands above your head.
2. Take a newspaper clipping out of your pocket and show it.
3. Lift something and show it.
4. Pound on the speaker's table to illustrate a point.
5. Recite a short verse.
6. Sing a line from a popular song.
7. Do a short demonstration. Show how your new mechanical pencil works.

Every one of those stunts is simple and easy to do. Try one of them in your next talk and note how it holds interest. Speeches need dramatizations of this kind. Look for them in your subject matter. If you can make a point by a demonstration, the point will be much more interesting to the audience than one that you make by speech alone. No matter how simple the stunt is, write out the stage directions. And don't assume that you can write those directions without trying to do the stunt. Try it first, then write it. Then rehearse it. Rehearse both words and actions until you can do them perfectly. A few of these stunts can add interest to what otherwise might be a rather dull speech.

18. Needle Your Facts

Data, at best, are dull. Yet nine out of ten speakers want to present figures. They want to startle the audience with some statistic, to juggle some data. If you are one of the nine, your problem is to make that data, those statistics, or those figures interesting. For no matter what kind of audience you have, they don't want to be bothered too much with information. They'll take a smattering of it unvarnished, and more of it if it is sugar-coated. But when you try to lay it on thick, they just can't take it.

And yet you have heard speakers throw data until the audience is punch drunk. Nobody knew what the man was saying and most of them doubted whether or not he knew.

Not long ago, after listening to a speaker, one of the audience said, "That fellow sure could quote figures."

"Do you remember any of them?" I asked.

"No, I don't," he replied.

Of what use was this man's data? Was it to give the impression that the speaker knew his stuff? Okay, if that was his purpose, he surely achieved it. But if he wanted to inform the audience, he surely failed in his point. He left nothing at all with them. If you plan to leave something with your audience, you had better give your data some life. How? Well, start with the premise that the data in your speech will be the dullest part. Then see what can be done to make it more interesting. Here are some suggestions.

1. *Don't Mind the Odd Cents*—When quoting figures, one good

rule is—don't mind the odd cents. Let's say you plan to explain that your business last year amounted to $3,364,392. Why not say "three million" or "three and one-third million," a figure which the listeners can picture quickly? All they'll remember, anyway, is three million, so why not write it that way? If you raised $1,017, why not write "over one thousand dollars"?

You may say, "Look, Hegarty, I want them to remember these figures exactly." That happens at times. But when you have that need, why not give them the figures in a printed piece. Then when you quote the figures you ask them to pick up the printed piece and go over it while you talk about it.

If you want to emphasize that amount over three and one-third million, you might say, "We did over three and one-third million. And you know how much over it was? Well, it was enough to buy a fleet of twelve bright, shiny, new Cadillacs." In making such a statement select an article on which they can readily figure the cost.

If you want to emphasize the seventeen dollars over the thousand in the club fund, you might say, "We raised over one thousand bucks. Do you know how much over? A buck twenty-five for every worker in this room."

Yes, figures are dull except to a figure filbert. You have to put some life into them when you talk to a general audience.

2. *Use as Few as Possible*—A second rule is—use as few figures as possible. If you want to show the growth of contributions to a fund over the last ten years, why quote the figures for each year? Why not say, "Here's what it was ten years ago. Here's what it was five years ago. Here's what it is today." Three figures they might remember. Give them the figures for each year and you put them to sleep.

It is common practice for speakers to quote columns of figures like those on the left of the next page. The same story can be told by a column like the one on the right. Just consider those two columns. Who but a memory expert could remember the long column?

879,942	1938			
987,481	1939			
1,217,110	1940			
1,418,218	1941		879,942	1938
1,729,346	1942		1,729,346	1942
1,890,765	1943		2,423,897	1947
1,976,923	1944			
2,189,657	1945			
2,356,965	1946			
2,423,897	1947			

Let's say these figures represent the business done. When you use the ten figures the group will probably remember the last one, perhaps the first if you emphasize something about it. But when you use only three figures, they might remember all three.

3. *Use a Chart*—Another way to make figures understood is to use a chart to illustrate them. But if you plan to use a chart, make it as simple as possible.

Not long ago a speaker asked my advice on a chart on which there were twelve columns of figures in one direction and ten columns in another. "They'll go to sleep when you show that," I advised him. We solved the problem by giving each member of the audience a copy of the chart, and then as the man on the stage told his story he asked them to make certain calculations on the charts they had.

The man who puts figures on his charts usually tries to put too much on one chart. Somehow men planning speeches, when advised to put part of their data on another chart, say, "I have twelve charts now. If I do what you say, I'll wind up with twenty or more."

My answer invariably is, "What's the difference? You are trying to explain, aren't you? And if it takes twenty or thirty charts to explain, use the twenty or more."

The fellow who makes your charts charges you by the time, and it makes little difference whether he spends an hour making one chart or three.

4. *Try Cartoons or Graphic Presentations*—If you have to use a chart, perhaps you can resort to cartoons to help get the idea over. A cartoon is easy to look at. It offers variety and helps hold the interest of an audience.

The other day we were discussing a set of charts that a man was to use. He said, "Put gremlins around those figures. I like gremlins." He did have a lot of figures and the gremlins helped make them interesting. So he got his gremlins.

Today there are companies that specialize in presenting figures graphically. You see these presentations in your trade magazines. Note them and study them. Perhaps they will give you an idea of what you can do with figures that you want to present.

Reports to stockholders of corporations use types of visual presentations that may be helpful. If you are stuck with figures to present, you can get help. Look for it and use it. I have seen speakers eliminate three or four pages of data in speech scripts. When I asked them why, they said, "Nobody is interested in that stuff." That is close to being true. But when you have the figures and have to present them, check to see what you can do graphically. You may find a helpful answer.

5. *Put Individuals in It*—Another way to handle this same thing is to put people in it. Let's say you quote the names of persons you and the audience know and tie them in with your data. That puts the information in a form that will be heard and perhaps remembered. I say "perhaps" because some minds just don't remember any figures.

Not long ago I was in Seattle, Washington. In a little guide of the city I read that in 1860 the population of Seattle was only 300. At the time I was there the town and surrounding area claimed over 400,000. I quoted that figure to a friend as we walked around window-shopping that night. "That's interesting," he said, "but my mind just doesn't remember figures like that." By talking about my friend, I can point up my story about figures—a population jump from nothing to almost a half a million in less than one hundred years.

You have heard illustrations that go, "It is enough money to feed all the people in China for one year." That is putting people into the figure but it does not mean too much to the audience. The group cannot imagine the number of people in China. If you can tag your figure on someone in the audience, you will do better. If you can say something like, "This money will support ten men like Jack here in the manner to which he has become accustomed— not for one year, or for two years, but for twenty years. Not Jack alone, but ten Jacks. Imagine spending that much money on a project like this."

Or you can say, "Your mayor in this town is paid $7,000 per year. The money for this project would support twenty mayors. Why, that's more money than this city puts out for the whole staff over at the city hall." By using an individual and his earnings, you are on common ground with your audience.

6. *Tell an Anecdote about the Figures*—Let's say you have written, "The government is going to spend twelve billion dollars on this project." Why not use a story to make that figure stick? Suppose you go out and ask ten people what twelve billion dollars means to them. You'll get a lot of different answers, that's certain. And on those answers you build your story. You talked to this man—that's a story. You know that stories are interesting. You said this, he said that—that's gossip. You know that gossip is interesting.

You have heard this kind of presentation of figures. I heard one man use it in a talk about government spending. He told the story about his survey. He related what the people said to him and what he said to them. Now many of the statements were humorous; those interviewed had little idea of what the big figure meant. The speaker used the story to illustrate his point that government spending cannot be reduced because the people who vote don't understand what it means to them. He could have made that statement. That is what most speakers would have done. Others might have tried to prove that it must be true because it is good common sense to believe that the public would get all steamed up if they knew how much the spending was costing them. But this speaker made a survey and he told a story about the survey and his story emphasized this ignorance. Because he handled the figure that way he got his point over.

There is a story in almost every figure. Remember the celebration your company had when they had the first million-dollar year? Tell about it. Then use that story to emphasize the fact that this year you did eleven million dollars. Tell about what John Whosis said when he was brought up to the front office to get the gold watch—your first employee with twenty-five years of continuous service. Today you have two hundred men with twenty-five years of service. Stories about little things and about big things can help point up your figures. Look about for these stories and write them in.

7. *Put the Audience in It*—Another plan is to put your figures in terms the man in the room can understand. You write, "Farm income in this country was twenty-six billion dollars last year." What does twenty-six billion dollars mean to me? I can't appreciate it—it's completely over my head. Yet you can get that figure into terms the audience can understand. Every listener has an income. Suppose you break that figure down into the average income per farm home. There are seven million farms in the United States. When you divide seven million into twenty-six billion you know that each farm has an income of about $3,700. That's about $300 per month or $10 per day. Now you are talking figures the average fellow can understand. He gets his pay per month or per week or per day. When you talk of $300 per month or $75 per week or $10 per day the man understands exactly what you are talking about. The twenty-six billion may be quite impressive, but the 75 bucks per week is something that any man can understand.

Similarly, if you wanted to make the point that most automobiles in the country are ten years old, make that statement, then ask, "How old is yours?"

You see this in the stories in the newspaper. The President submits a request for an appropriation. That night the papers say,

"That means four hundred dollars for every individual in the country." You read that, you whistle, and immediately you start figuring. You have a wife and two kids—that's four. Four times four—you whistle again. Your share is sixteen hundred bucks. Too much.

The President asked for billions. The figure he used was too large for you to understand. But that four hundred bucks per person is understandable and impressive. Many speakers quote figures that are away over the heads of the group. They could avoid that by taking the trouble to apply them to each member of the audience. Almost any figure can be reduced to terms that have a meaning to the listeners. Determine what those terms are and then get at the reducing. Here are some examples:

The fund wants to raise $300,000. You can talk about that amount until you are blue in the face, but I sit there asking, "How much from me?" Let's say there are one thousand prospective donors—that means $300 per giver, doesn't it?

The sales department sets a quota of 50,000 units. There are 800 salesmen. Okay, that means sixty-three units per salesman, doesn't it?

The market has 10,000 families. Experience shows that three out of every ten families buy the product. Then you have three thousand prospects in this market. But if you are trying to get somebody to do something about three thousand prospects, you are talking about too large a figure. So let's break it down some more. Let's take it in blocks—city blocks. There are forty families in every block. That means there are twelve prospects in every block. Now you have a figure that can be understood.

Some figures can be reduced easily. Others take more thought. But it will pay you to look for your best answer to that question, "How much for me?"

8. *Let Them Help*—Many times you can make your data stick by having the audience help you add or subtract or multiply. Let's say you want to add two figures. You write down the figures, draw the line under them, and ask the audience to give you the answer. This centers all attention on the figures.

There are a number of tricks that you can do with figures when you are giving a talk with a blackboard or chart pad. You can have one of the audience come up and write down the figures for you. This gets attention for your figures, for the others in the audience will watch carefully to see if your blackboard man makes any mistakes. On top of that they feel they are helping because the man selected is one of them.

When you want to get attention for a figure you can ask the audience to give you estimates. Tell them:

"Last year we sold one hundred thousand of these appliances. That was our sales—one hundred thousand. How many of them do you think came back for service?"

Ask one man to guess. Write his guess on the blackboard. Ask another, then another. Now you have them in a game. When you have a number of guesses, write the true figure on the board.

By letting them help you with the figures, you make the figures interesting. All audiences like to help. As Jimmy Durante says, "Everybody wants to get into the act."

9. *Personalize*—You can try to put your figure in terms of one man. Instead of saying that your business represents so much in retail sales, you might say this: "Every five minutes one thousand persons somewhere in the U.S.A. walk up to a counter in a retail store and buy one of these gadgets."

Your audience can understand one man, a number of men, a crowd of men. These are in their experience. The gadgets bought by the people mentioned above amount to about one hundred thousand per day. That would be about thirty million per year. Those are impressive figures. They are the kind that most speakers use. But let's list these figures in a column and see which explains best:

Thirty million per year
One hundred thousand per day
One thousand every five minutes
Two hundred every minute
Three every second

Those are the figures. To personalize them you put persons in them, thus:

Every year thirty million men walk up to a counter and. . . .
Every day one hundred thousand men walk. . . .
Every five minutes one thousand men walk up. . . .
Every minute two hundred men walk up. . . .
Every second three men walk up. . . .

Does putting the men in help? Well, it does give a picture. When I say, "Thirty men walk into a store," you see a crowd of men going through the revolving doors of the store, don't you? If I say "three every minute," I do not give you that picture. So by personalizing the figures we present the figure and we give a picture to go with it.

Some thought should be given to that picture. You must decide what you want the listeners to see. What picture will best help you make your point?

Let's say the figure is 39,000. You want to make the point that last year 39,000 residential buildings were destroyed by fire. There are good picture possibilities in that figure. The homes are picturesque, fire is picturesque, fire engines running to fires are picturesque.

You can picture all those buildings in one town, a town of about 125,000 population.

You can picture the tenants out in the cold—125,000 of them.

You can picture the houses on fire and the tenants running from them.

You can picture the fire engines running to those fires, how many, how often, the firemen hanging from the rushing vehicles.

10. *Localize Your Figures*—Always try to use figures that apply locally. Don't use national figures if you can help it. The man in the audience is more likely to understand the figures for his county than for the three thousand counties in the United States. Better still, use his city or his section of the city.

Often the advertising speaker talks of national circulation of magazines. The figures would be just as interesting if he used the local circulation of those magazines. Why tell a salesman or a store owner that 30,000,000 people will see the advertising when there are only 200,000 people in his territory?

Why not talk only of that 200,000? Explain that out of that 200,000 people, 72,000 will see the advertising—seven out of every twenty. Then he has something to go on. Ask the store owner to stand at the door of his store and count twenty people passing by. Tell him that seven of that twenty will see the advertising. That is speaking his language. He knows where the front door of his store is. He knows those people walking by. Your advertising is talking to seven out of twenty of them. What are his thoughts? Couldn't they logically be, "Well, then, I had better do something to let those seven know that I handle your line?"

If you want to tell your audience of the loss in this country from floods or erosion or any other carelessness, use the national figure if you think it will help. But add the local figure too. Tell them how much it cost their state or their county or their town. Localize the figures and you will add interest.

11. *Repeat the Basis*—When using a chart of figures that require some time in explanation, repeat the basis of your comparison. If you are using industry figures, remind them that these are industry and not company figures. If you are using national figures, keep reminding the group that the figures are national. Try for originality. If you hit a new idea, you'll certainly attract attention. With a little imagination you should be able to get yourself certain devices that will work well for you.

Always try to bring your comparisons down to the people in the room. The amount of money would buy enough cigarettes to do him for the rest of his life or all the clothes he'll need for the next ten years. That's what I mean—get it down close to the chair he's sitting in. Make it personal and he will listen and understand.

Yes, when you have data to present, put it in the most interesting form you can work out and eliminate those frills that will make it uninteresting. Perhaps you might have to sacrifice some of the information in the interest of making the audience understand. But don't worry. They can take only so much in one dose.

When you try to lay it on, they miss some. That's why it's best to handle your material in such a way that they retain some of it.

Always remember that when you have data to present, the data will be the dullest part of your talk. It may be dramatic and exciting to you and perhaps to some of the listeners. But to most of them—no. They want as little of it as possible. That's why you should put the heaviest work on making it interesting. Let's get down on paper the rest of your talk. Then let's take the data section and get to work on that.

Perhaps you may feel you are tricking the audience when you doll up your data, but that's not the point. You are giving it to them the way they want it. Just like the medicine in the capsule or the bitter pill inside the sugar-coating. What's more, you are helping them understand and retain it.

If your data is not too important, don't use it. If you must use it, simplify it and try to make it interesting.

Let's check the methods for making your figures interesting.

1. Remember that your data will be the dullest part of your talk. If you don't need it, leave it out.
2. Use as few figures as possible.
3. Drop off the odd cents. Use round numbers—three hundred—three thousand—three million.
4. Charts can help you clarify the figures. When you show them, you give the audience two chances to understand—through seeing and through hearing.
5. Investigate what you can do with the graphic methods of presentation. Cartoons are popular—use them if possible.
6. Put individuals into the figures. Have men, women, and children running around in the figures and you add interest.
7. Tell anecdotes about the figures. All of us like a story.
8. Put the audience into the figures. Present the figures in terms the audience can compare with what they know. So much per day, so much per week, so much per family.
9. Let them help. Ask for their help. Let them call out the answers, let them write on the blackboard.

10. Personalize the figures. Every day ten men walk up. . . .
11. Localize the figure if you can. Talk about my town, my ward, my precinct, my back yard.
12. Repeat the basis. Make sure the audience understands that the figures are for my ward, my precinct.

But let me repeat—if your data are not too important, don't use them. If you must use them, simplify them, reduce them, try to make them interesting.

19. Now Let's Check the Script

If you have followed the directions thus far, you have the makings of a good speech. You have thought out what you are going to cover, you have written a synopsis, you have dug up the material and laid it out on paper. You have selected a plan of presentation, you have laid out the parts as units, and you have written the end of the opus.

That is about all a man needs to do in writing a speech. If you have followed all the suggestions, you have the framework of a good speech, a speech that your listeners will like. For you are using the anecdote, you are using gossip, you have introduced the news element, you have references to people, live people, the kind that the audience likes to hear about. You have talked about your possessions, you have used dramatization, and you have made your data or facts interesting.

Yes, you have a speech that should go over well. But don't start practicing yet. There is another job to do. Let's check the material you have written. And it does need checking. If you have followed the suggestions, this speech of yours will, no doubt, ring the bell. But even so, it can stand some pointing up. Remember, anything you can do you can do better. The following chapters list some of the checks you might make and explain how the checks can be made.

20. Check for Variety

Now that the speech is written, let's check it over for variety. The proverb says, "Variety is the spice of life." Variety helps make your speech good. The vaudeville show illustrates what I mean. First you saw dancers, then elephants, then singers, then acrobats —one following the other, not two teams of dancers together. You always wondered what was coming next. Try for a speech organization that keeps your audience asking, "What's coming next?"

It is easy to plan for variety. So far in this book we have discussed a number of different types of speech material. Remember those devices for making a talk interesting.

1. The anecdote	5. Persons and names
2. Gossip	6. News
3. Needling your facts	7. The family
4. Dramatics	8. Your possessions

Your check for variety in this talk should determine how well you have shuffled the elements. Don't put all your stories together, or all your facts, or all your personalities and names. Shuffle them. Perhaps you are not using all the elements, but if you use only three or four, shuffle the three or four so that you have variety. If you have two stories together, try to separate them.

Try for variety also in the types of material you use. All your stories do not have to be about the same kind of characters. The audience might go for one story about your Johnny, who is four years old and bright as a tack, but two or three or four stories about Johnny might be a pain. In my talk on "How to Run a

Sales Meeting" I use stories on these subjects: "A Fight in the Movies," "The Chairman of a Meeting," "My Number Two Son," "An Indian," "A Sales Training Meeting," "The Speaker Who Shuffled His Card Notes," "A Janitor," "The Fellow Who Passed Out Something for the Audience to Look at," "A Waiter," "A Colored Fellow," "An Irish Judge," "The Fellow Who Is Called Upon without an Idea."

Because this talk is about running a meeting, many of the illustrations must be about speakers and meetings. But as you look over that list you can see how the one element, the anecdote, can be changed to give variety.

Your stories should be varied as to locale, characters, and types of conversation. Don't use a bartender in all your stories; it might lead people to think that you hang around bars. Use cops, ministers, bellhops, taxi drivers, too. Show that you get around. If both your good stories are about bartenders, change one to make the hero a taxi driver. If the settings of two stories are the same, change one of them. What difference does it make whether it is a drugstore or a bar and grill? You may say, "Look, I am seldom in such low places as bars and grills." Okay, use other locales. Don't try to make an audience feel that you are at home in Leo's Place if you never go into such a joint. Use the Union League Club instead—but don't place your story in the Union League Club if your club activities are confined to the Mulligan Marching and Chowder Club. Remember this—a story is usually just as good regardless of the type of characters or the locale. Put it in your everyday environment.

That next element is conversation. Here you have the same problem you do in the anecdote. You may wonder why I differentiate between the anecdote and gossip. I separate the two because I feel that the man writing a speech should think of the anecdote and the conversation that builds up the anecdote as two things. So many stories used by speakers are dead because they are not built up with conversation. So as you look over the conversation in your speech, check it for characters, for dialect, for what is said. Are any of these factors too much alike? If so, change them

and you will come closer to that variety that makes speeches
sparkle.

Now for your facts, your statistics. Chapter 18 gives you ten or
more ways to make facts interesting. Still, as you put the speech
down on paper, you find you have four facts that you want the
audience to remember—but what have you done? You have handled all of them alike. The other day a speaker said to me, "This
speech of mine is lousy with statistics." Later I listened to him
give the speech and I had to admit that it was. But he had made
no effort to make those statistics interesting. With a little work,
any speaker can make his statistics more palatable.

Here is what I mean:

Present your first fact unadulterated without the sugar-coating,
thus—"There are a million Elliths in the United States."

That's one way, but don't handle the other facts in the same way.
Try building the second up with a story, like this:

"The other day I said to a friend, '62 per cent of the Elliths in
the U.S.A. are rumpus.' He said, 'I wouldn't believe it. But that is
true. Think of that, 62 per cent are rumpus.' "

In this way you put the facts into a story. You might go on to
explain what you said about it when you first heard the figure,
what the man in the other audience said, what your secretary said.
That would be using gossip to build up the fact.

Present the third fact in connection with a news item in the
morning's newspaper: "I saw this item in the newspaper this morning. I cut it out. Here is what it said, 'The purchasing power of the
Elliths has increased 100 per cent in the past year.' Think of that.
They're in a position to buy twice as much as they were one year
ago."

Connect your fourth fact with a name:

"I was talking to John Henry and John told me—" John Henry
is one of the audience, someone the audience knows, thus your
fact will have added interest.

There are four ways, each different, and if your talk presents
a number of facts try this variety in your presentation.

Then, too, you can vary your dramatics. Did you ever study the gestures you use when you make a speech? I did a talk not long ago, and it was a custom of the club to have a photographer snap the speaker in action. This fellow got a shot of me with my hand above my head. My friends who see that photograph on my office wall say, "Ed, you sure were giving it to them when they snapped that." Now if I had ever been asked to testify under oath as to whether or not I ever raised my hand above my head when before an audience I would have said, "No, I never do." And I would be speaking the truth as I know it. Yet there was the photograph to testify that I did raise my hand.

By changing your gestures you get some variety. I have one friend who shakes his finger at the audience—it is about his only gesture. When you tell him about it, he says, "Yes, I know, and I have tried to break myself of it. It's a carry-over from my old school-teaching days." Now one gesture is not good. A little practice will get you some variety in the gestures you use. But this variety should be planned, and it should be written into the script. At this point you pound the table, at this you stand on your head. Now you whistle, now you sing a bar. Now you tear your hair. Now you wave your arms. Then you let those arms hang limp at your sides.

You say you can't do any of those things. You say you plan to stand up there and start speaking and keep going until you can sit down. No, no, not that. Sample these dramatics—a gesture or two. You'll find you won't drop dead. Try one in this speech, two in the next, three in the next, and so on. Now walk three steps slowly. Now stand still. When you demonstrate a machine, stand on one side for a part of the demonstration, then move to the other side. Turn the machine around, move it forward, move it back. That movement gives the variety that audiences like. Try for it in everything you do.

You can also get variety in the names of persons that you mention. In the audience there may be many of your friends. If so, you can mention this one and that one without repeating. But many times you know nobody in the audience—perhaps you have seen none of them before. Usually, though, somebody has arranged for your appearance, and you can mention that person and the chairman. But don't mention one person a number of times. He may like it but the others may not. Try for variety in the persons you talk about.

You can get variety in the news you bring in to help prove your points. Don't take it all from the financial page of the newspaper. There are the news pages, and the home page, and the society page, and the comics, and the classified sections. There is news and a tie-in with your subject in all of them. Then don't overlook the advertisements. They, too, are news. Ever notice the pages that your wife spends the time on? They are the advertising pages. Chapter 14 gives you many suggestions on how to make news interesting. But don't treat all your news alike. Vary it.

Just look at that list of sources of news on page 95 and you will see the great opportunity you have to get variety in the news you use. Pick one item out of the newspaper, one out of a magazine, the next out of a feature of your plan, now something unusual, follow this with a bit of research, now a bit about a pet worry, then a minute on some peeve, wind up with a statement that reveals some knowledge you have which the audience does not have. Each of these items is news. Cover them as they are listed and you have a variety of subject matter.

There is also that wonderful source of speech material—your family. Even though your family consists of one wife, period, you have her family and your family. Those in-laws and uncles and aunts, and the cousins on your mother's side, twice removed. All of them are good. There is no need to use any of them more than once. You have the rich uncle, and the lying uncle, and the drinking uncle, and the temperance uncle, and so on far into the night. Even though Uncle Joe is the only one that speaks English, even though he is the one that is always getting off the wisecracks, you can attribute some of his wit to Uncle Gus, who is always clicking his store teeth.

But it is not good to use only uncles. You might use an uncle, a cousin, a father-in-law. When you use the family, vary the personnel.

Your possessions give you another wide field for variety. Don't tell a number of stories about Rover, the dog. Tell one about Tiny, the canary, or Daisy, the cat. Not long ago I heard a speaker tell a story about Wowo, the goldfish that had been bought as a birthday present for his little girl. Your 1940 car may be good for a number of stories, but one will be about right. Change the other one to the boy's bicycle or toy airplane. You have so many possessions to talk about that you should have no trouble varying the subject matter. All are good, but not an overdose of any one, please.

Of course you can get by with a talk that is all anecdote, one story after another, but it is better to vary the methods you use. Use all the devices. First an anecdote, then some gossip, then a fact, now some dramatics—then start that routine all over again. That's the idea. Get this kind of variety into the script and it will be more interesting.

In your method of speaking you can also have variety. You can speak fast and then speak slowly. You can change the speed with which you cover certain parts of the subject. Now you talk in the vernacular, now in your Sunday English. Vary the feeling, the intensity.

By changing the volume of your voice, by whispering now and shouting later, by screaming, by weeping you can get variety. You may say, "I can't do things like that." Perhaps you can't. But if you plan to do any of them, for goodness' sake don't have all the shouting coming at one time. Shout a little in this part and then again later on.

Some speakers are good at reciting poetry. That gives a welcome variety—if it is done well. One time I needed a special ending for a speech and I wrote a poem. It was probably a poor poem, but I got so many requests from the audience for copies that I leave poetry alone. A prayer also offers variety. It brings a change in pace, an intensity of feeling not to be found in other material.

There is another kind of variety that should be mentioned, although it will be covered more fully in later chapters. It is variety in your writing. Let's say you are fond of long sentences. Long sentences don't speak too well. Your script will be a better speaking vehicle if you vary the length of your sentences, now a long one, now a short one.

Not long ago one of my friends heard me make my speech "How to Run a Meeting." Watching the performance, he said, "You know you had something doing every minute—and it was something different." Now most listeners wouldn't have noticed. They would have liked the talk because of the variety and because of the change of pace but they wouldn't have understood exactly how it was done. And they would never have dreamed that all of it was planned—all of it written out. Since you have the talk written in units, it's rather easy to scatter the various devices for giving variety. If you seem to have it, okay. If not, do the rewriting or rearranging necessary. The audience likes variety, so write it into the script. Keep them asking, "What's coming next?"

You can look for variety in the words you use. Do you have a habit of using one word too often? I know that I had a habit of overworking the word "lots." My scripts were full of "lots of this," "a lot of times," "I do that a lot." One day in checking a script I got out the thesaurus and found that there were at least twenty-five words that could be substituted on occasions. Here is the list I gathered:

many: numerous, a quantity of, profusion
host: legion, swarms, bushels, bevy
flock: herds, covey, crowd, gang, army
number: several, few, some, multitude
company: array, display, multiplicity
sundry: divers

Yes, there is no reason to use one word over and over again. You might get to be like the Negro preacher who so fancied the word "tremendous" and used it so often that his flock called him "Tremendous" Jones.

Let's review the ways you can get variety:

1. Have you varied your stories as to characters, locale?
2. The conversation—is it too much of the same?
3. The data—have you made use of the devices available to make them interesting?
4. The gestures you plan—are they alike?
5. How about the persons you bring in—is there a variety of characters?
6. Are you making any member of your family work too much?
7. Your possessions—there is not too much of any one of them, is there?
8. Are you varying the news you use?
9. What stunts do you plan? If you have more than one stunt, are they different?
10. How about your methods of speaking. Do you have the shouting lines, the whispering lines?
11. Have you thought of a bit of poetry, or a prayer?
12. Are your sentences varied—short and long?
13. How about a change of pace—now fast, now slow?
14. How about words—do you use the same word over and over again?

21. Cut Out the "We's"

It is quite natural when you write your speech to overwork the word "we." That is almost the rule if it is a business speech. "We built this factory," "We turned out this production," "We made this many sales," "We did this amount of advertising." We did this. We did that. When I am asked to revise a speaking script, I usually find that one of the most difficult jobs is getting out the "we's."

Of course there are times when the "we's" should be used and times when they should come out. Let's discuss a few of both.

"We's" should come out when:

1. They make it sound as if you are bragging.
2. You are expressing your own opinion.
3. You could say "you" and give the credit to the audience.

"We's" belong in when:

1. They include the audience.
2. You are telling stories about yourself.

Often a simple change in wording can eliminate the "we's." Here is a paragraph from an advertising talk. There are a lot of "we's" in it and they don't seem to help. They seem to put the speaker in the position of taking too much credit, if not bragging:

> We feel that is the job of our magazine, radio and other national advertising. We feel we've got a preselling job to do. If we can presell the customers, if we can get them into the dealers' stores, we have gone a long way toward wrapping up the sale.

149

There are six "we's" in those forty-nine words. Now let's see what happens when all of them are cut out:

> That's the job of our magazine, radio and other national advertising. It has a preselling job to do. If it can presell customers, if it can get them into dealers' stores, it has gone a long way toward wrapping up the sale.

The revision gives the credit to the advertising and not to us. But won't that paragraph be a better speaking script?

Many speakers have the habit of using "I" or "we" so that it sounds as if the man is speaking his own opinion. He states what everybody knows to be a fact, but his wording implies that the fact is his opinion. Now it is nice for his opinion to agree with the facts, but the listener is left wondering. Here are some examples of what I mean in the column at the left. The column at the right shows how the same statement could be made without the "I" or "we."

I would like to tell you. . . .	You will be glad to hear. . . .
It means this to me. . . .	It means this to you. . . .
I take pleasure in telling you. . . .	You will be glad to know. . . .
Here's what I mean. . . .	This means. . . .
I feel this is important. . . .	This is important. . . .
I talked them into. . . .	They agreed to. . . .

There is not much difference in the meaning of the statements on the right, but the audience gets a different idea of the speaker. This fellow is talking sense. It is natural, of course, for a speaker to make statements like those in the left-hand column. That is how we talk. But remember, we agreed to write this speech in terms of the other fellow's interest. That is what we are trying for when we make such changes.

There are times when the "we" you dictated or wrote could be changed to "you" without any trouble or without any change in meaning.

Not so long ago an associate brought a script of a talk for me to look over. His first line was: "We put on 364 schools." His department had furnished the instructors, the training aids, and the other properties used in putting on the schools. But the schools are put on in towns all over the country and the local representatives had arranged for the places, had invited the guests, and had promoted the school in many ways.

Since this talk was being made to the fellows who had helped put on the schools, I suggested that the first line be changed to, "This past year 364 schools were put on." Now the speaker didn't claim all the credit. The other fellow could figure that he, too, did some work on the operation. My friend's script would have been even better if he had said, "You put on 364 schools." He could have said that without stretching the truth. Telling them that they had put on the schools would have been a gracious gesture. If my friend had said that, the reaction of the audience would have been, "Wait a minute, you did a lot too. If it hadn't been for you, we couldn't have had those sessions."

Here is an example of how "we" can be changed to "you," with benefit to the script. Let's say you are the representative of a manufacturer. You are speaking to a group of salesmen who sell your product. You say:

> We have the best engineering, we have the best design, we have the best styling. We have the best construction, we have the best performance, we have the best pricing policy. Added to that, we have the best advertising, we have the best display, we have the best deal to sell.

Now that is an exaggeration, but it is the way we are inclined to use "we" in our presentations. Now if those salesmen are selling your product, why couldn't you write that paragraph thus:

> When you sell this product, you have the best engineering, you have the best design, you have the best styling. You have the best construction, you have the best performance. You have the best pricing system. Then added to all that you have the best advertising, you have the best display, you have the best deal to sell.

The speaker may still sound as if he is bragging, but he is bragging about what they have, not about what he has or what his factory has done. It is difficult to build up the pride of those salesmen in what his factory has done. But he can build their pride in the line they have to sell. For it is *their* line—it belongs to them.

There is a big difference. It doesn't take much persuasion to show you which is the better of those two passages. That same sort of transition can be made when you are talking about your club, your community fund, your pet charity, or any other project. Don't speak of the activity as if it belonged to you or to the board of directors. Speak of it as if it belonged to the listeners. You don't run it; they run it. You are not proud of it; they are proud of it. Get the idea?

Some subjects are difficult to handle in that way. It is not always easy to find a tie-in with the interest of the audience. But search for it. Almost any talk can be written so that it appeals directly to the listener. If you think about it, you can cut out the "we," substitute "you," and strengthen the appeal.

Now I said that there are times when "we" is right. Here is a paragraph from a speech given to a group of sales managers. "We" is used a lot in the paragraph, but this time the "we" includes the audience. By "we" the speaker means "you and I":

> We look into the future. We see many changes coming. We will see the greatest period of penny pinching that we have ever seen. We are going to have to meet those changes. We are going to have to do something about them.

Now those "we's" I wouldn't cut. They are all right as they are. In using them the speaker is including his audience in the "we." He is telling what they have to do together. This is a kind of "we" that belongs in your script.

Another time that "we" belongs is when you are telling a story. Most times the story is on yourself and you will be using "I" instead of "we." Never start a story, "A fellow who lives in my town was making a trip from Los Angeles to San Francisco. . . ." Start that story, "I was going from Los Angeles to San Francisco. . . ." The audience will like it better. You may say, "But it didn't happen to me, it happened to my neighbor." All right, I still insist, let it happen to *you* in the story. The exception would be if the story makes you out a hero; then it would be all right to use the other fellow. (I make this point in Chap. 12, but I am repeating it here because I don't want you to get the idea that the ban on "we" and "I" applies to the story too.)

Here is a passage with a lot of "we's" in it. Perhaps they belong, perhaps they do not. I suggest that you go through it and make the changes that will make it a better speaking script. (This talk is to be made by a manufacturer's representative to salesmen who sell his product):

> Naturally one model does not make a line, so we have a complete line to show you. This is the first meeting we have held to present a new line where we did not give you a lot of facts and figures. But there is one trend that we want to talk about, one fact we want you to consider.

How would you rewrite that paragraph to make it a good talking script?

Here is another example that you can check in the same way. (Talk by a sales manager to other sales managers in an industry conference):

> We have to take a broad outlook on this. We have to analyze what the job is, break it into its parts. We have to break down each part into tasks. Then we have to develop a plan for teaching those tasks as a part of that job. That is our job. We have to do it. We can't delegate it. We have to tackle it ourselves.

There are a lot of "we's," aren't there? What are you going to do about them?

Now here are a number of statements. Some should be changed, some should be left as they are. Which should be changed?

> Next year we will produce
> We plan to make
> We do most of our training by mail

We are now carrying on
We were visiting a plant
In our business we have this advantage
We furnish our men with
When I write to John or Henry
Here is something we mail out to prospects
I would like to tell you
I think this is interesting

These are eleven types of passages that get into speeches. In fact, I have taken all of them from the printed proceedings of a meeting.

To sum up, here is a guide to what should be in and what should come out:

1. All "we's" should come out when they make you sound like a braggart, a wise guy, or a know-it-all.
2. Cut out all "I's" and "we's" when you are expressing your own opinion. If it is the opinion of your company or your group, attribute it to them.
3. When you can say "you" and give the credit to the other fellow, do it. Always express the idea in terms of his interest, not yours.
4. Leave the "we's" in when they include the audience.
5. When you are telling stories, leave the "I" and "we" in. That's especially true when you get the worst of the deal or the joke is on you. When the joke is on the other fellow, use him in the story. Don't make yourself a hero.

22. Check for Clarity

Now let's check for clarity. Let's see if your audience will understand what you are saying. Perhaps your speech reads beautifully; perhaps the English is excellent. You've used the proper words in the proper places. Then, as you rattle it off, the sound of your voice may fascinate you. But will your audience understand what you mean?

Here is a paragraph I copied from a talk given by a sales-manager friend of mine:

> Today we enjoy a favorable position in this business. But there is danger that we may have grown too complacent. Knowledge that stems from experience warns us that even today we may be jeopardizing our position, through stultifying inaction. Considered from the objective viewpoint, there is no primrose path ahead. To preclude disaster, we need an active prosecution of the business from all angles.

That sounds good, doesn't it? I know the fellow who used that and I'll bet he went to a dictionary and dug up some of those words. And what was the result? Fog, and more fog.

Let's analyze that paragraph and try to determine what the speaker meant: He had a number of ideas that he put together. Let's list them:

1. His company had a favorable position in the business.
2. They might grow complacent.
3. Some past experience warned them that because they were doing nothing, they might be jeopardizing their position.
4. There was no primrose path ahead.
5. They had to start after business.

Even when the five thoughts are written out in simple sentences
the idea is still not clear. You may say, "It is a poor paragraph." I
admit that it is. But it is out of a speech, and it illustrates the kind
of stuff so many speakers write into speeches. It might be made
much clearer by this revision:

> We are leaders in this business. And we didn't get to be leaders
> by doing nothing. But that's what we are doing now—not a thing.
> And what happens to any company that does nothing? They start
> slipping. Even now we may have started to slip. And there's only
> one way to stop that slipping. We have to realize the days of milk
> and honey are over. We've got to get to work. We've got to work
> hard. We've got to work every angle—go after the business with
> all we have and all we know.

Here is another gem that I wrote down:

> Yet I think that I have sensed in more than one businessman a cer-
> tain distrust of the profit appeal when it is used too broadly, too
> bluntly, too monotonously—that is, when it is not used skillfully.

Can you make anything out of that passage? How can you use
the profit appeal too broadly? How can you use the profit appeal
too bluntly? How can you use the profit appeal too monotonously?
How can you use the profit appeal skillfully?

Now that last question could get you an answer. But the others?
I don't get the meaning. The person who wrote that in his speech
probably thought it was mighty good. When he read it to himself he was quite proud of it. When he read it to the ever-loving
wife he mistook her slight frown for approbation. When he rehearsed, it sounded good as he said it aloud. But what in the world
does it mean?

Here's what you might look for in checking your own manuscript for clarity:

1. Sentences and paragraphs that don't mean anything or that
   will confuse the hearer.
2. Words of doubtful meaning—the words that professional
   people bandy about so easily.

3. Trade terms that may not be clear to your audience.
4. Technical jargon that may not be understood.
5. Explanations that may not be clear.

When you come to a passage that may be in any way confusing, ask yourself, "Will they understand?"

Then let's check for those words of doubtful meaning. I don't mean words that are not familiar to you. I am speaking of words that are sprinkled through speeches—words that the audience might not know. You may say, "When you view the situation objectively. . . ." You may understand the word "objectively" but does the audience understand? One of my friends put a young man in his organization on the job of interviewing applicants for positions. His instructions to the young man were, "You have to view everybody objectively." To my friend that instruction was simple. To the boy it had an entirely different meaning. My friend didn't find this out for about a week, until he sent another employee over to ask the young fellow how he was getting along.

The young fellow said he was getting along fine. The second man asked him what he had learned.

The young fellow said, "There is one thing I've learned about this job. I surely have to be objectionable."

There is a whole list of such words that seem to be popular with speechmakers. You hear such words as these:

integrate	empirical	functional
dissemble	subjective	abstract
prescient	sardonic	vertical
horizontal	persiflage	recreant
moribund	implement	

I made notes of these words as speakers said them. It is not a list that I made up or a list of words that I don't like. They are good words but not good for a speech. Any one of them may express your meaning, but will the listeners understand?

I heard a speaker use the word "empirical" one night in a speech. He said, "Empirically speaking. . . ." There were six men at the table with me and I asked each one of them what the word meant.

Each gave me a different definition. The next morning I looked up the word in the large dictionary. It did have a number of meanings. I met the speaker later that day and asked him what he meant when he used the word. He said, "Rule of thumb." Now why didn't he say "rule of thumb"? It would have been clear, and every one of his listeners would have understood.

With a little thought you can express the same idea in words that anybody will understand. The words listed are seven-letter words or better, but there are also a large number of small words that are just as unsuitable. Words like prone, prior, vapid, facet, tacit are all good words but others will make your meaning clearer in a speech.

Next check for technical language. If the audience is to be made up of technical men, technical language will be all right, for presumably it will be understood. But if the talk is to be given to the Rotary or the Kiwanis or any of the other service clubs, steer clear of the technical. You know how you get tangled up with technical language, how you always have to pause to figure out whether the podiatrist or the pediatrician is the foot doctor. The audience is in the same position when you use the technical language of your profession. Financial words come under this heading, and legal words and the words of doctors and medicine. If you belong to any of those professions, watch that you do not go technical on your audience.

Here's a quotation I took from a speech I heard recently. The speaker was talking about the rating of salesmen. He said, "First you rate the qualitative factor, then the quantitative." Now I imagine that was mighty plain to the speaker but I have spent most of my life in the business of selling and sales management and it meant not a thing at all to me.

Perhaps it is not clear because the idea is not completely expressed. It may be that the speaker was trying to express his idea too fast. It may be that he didn't allow himself enough words. But no matter what the trouble. I am sure that most of his listeners lost his point.

Many times this desire to save words results in thoughts that are not clearly expressed. Here is a line from a talk describing a refrigerator:

> The horizontal motif of the decorative lines eliminates the lanky look apparent in some competitive models and conforms to the horizontal feeling of the modern kitchen.

The sentence describes some horizontal lines on the front of the refrigerator. The lines make the refrigerator look wider than it is. Then these lines match the horizontal lines of the floor cabinets in the modern kitchen. As speech material that sentence might better be written:

> See these horizontal lines across this door? They make the refrigerator look wider—not tall and skinny like so many refrigerators today. Another thing about them—they match the horizontal lines on everything else in the kitchen—stove, cabinets, and sink.

Revised in that way the idea is expressed more clearly. Sometimes you can't cut the wordage too thin. If you speak your thought too fast, the idea may be lost. In checking for clarity, see if you have any sentences like this refrigerator example in which you went so fast that the idea was lost along the way. It is easy to do. No matter how hard you try to write your speech in spoken language, you will have trouble doing a complete job.

Let's say that passage was written in direct statements. It would go something like this:

> These decorative lines are horizontal. They eliminate the lanky look of competitive models. They match the horizontal lines of the modern kitchen.

In Chap. 8 I made the point that introductory phrases and dangling phrases are not good speech material. Look at that sentence as it was originally written. Make sentences out of those introductory and dangling phrases, and the passage is easier to understand. It becomes three sentences instead of one. But it speaks better as three sentences than it does as one.

There is a lot of this fast writing in the "How to Use" or the "How to Install" directions that come with most products. The writer does not give enough details. The humorous writers and the cartoonists have a lot of fun with such directions. And well they might. Now if the man who writes the directions telling you how to use his product cannot make himself clear to you, don't you see how careful you should be to make things clear to your audience?

Trade jargon can be confusing, even to men who work at the trade. I love to hear the sales management consultants get off such bits of nothing as "sales casting," "inflationary cycles," "areas of influence," "distributive control." They leave me cold, and a bit confused, too. An automobile salesman calls a car a "job." Why? I don't know. The public calls it an automobile or a car.

Even the simplest of trade language may be misunderstood. A salesman sold a refrigerator to a homemaker. When he had finished giving her the explanation of what the refrigerator would do, he asked her, "Now is there anything you don't understand?"

The woman said, "Yes, I don't quite understand about defrosting."

The salesman said, "Why, that's easy. Just cut it off."

A month later the salesman met the woman. He asked her how her refrigerator was working and how she liked it. The woman said, "I like it all except defrosting."

"Defrosting," the salesman said. "Why that's simple. What do you find difficult about it?"

"Well," the woman said, "there must be some easier way to get the ice off than to cut it off with a knife."

The salesman had meant that she should turn off the electricity when she wanted to defrost. To him that was "cutting it off." To her, "cutting it off" meant getting a knife from the kitchen cabinet and cutting the ice off the freezer. Yes, even simple technical language should be checked.

So check through your talk. Are you making yourself clear, or are you mouthing words that sound all right but mean nothing? Here are some guides:

1. Check for sentences or paragraphs that are not clear.
2. Look for wording that might confuse.
3. Check out the words of doubtful meaning; substitute words that we all know.
4. Eliminate trade words that may not be clear to the audience.
5. Blue-pencil the technical jargon that may not be understood.
6. Check to see that all explanations explain. Remember the directions on the package.

23. Is It Specific?

Of course they want to "broaden their horizons." But if you have written that in your speech, let's cut it out. Let's substitute for "broaden their horizons" whatever it is they should do. Perhaps you mean to learn to speak in public, to learn to dance divinely, to learn to answer the waiter in perfect French, to master the manly art of fisticuffs. If so, say that. Be specific. Be definite. Be particular. Be precise.

Any of the skills listed in the paragraph above could be listed under the head of "broadening their horizons," but when you mention them by name the audience understands. If you listen to as many speeches as I do, you will be conscious of the great amount of vague generalities that an otherwise sensible citizen gives out when he stands up to talk. As much as I watch myself, I find myself needing a second sentence to explain a preceding one that was a little vague. So let's check to see if we can make this talk more specific, more precise.

There are a number of ways that you can fail to be specific. Let's discuss a few of them:

There is the method of expressing your ideas. You say some words. In themselves the words are all right, but they don't express the ideas concretely.

There are the times when we weaken the statement by trying to include too much. We don't say what we mean specifically because we feel that a small percentage of the listeners might be left out.

Then we tack on additions. We say, "etc." Perhaps that addition is not needed. We may have covered all the ideas in what we said before the "etc."

The names of places is another point on which we are seldom definite. We say, "A large eastern city. . . ."

Next come dates and times. Somehow we have built up a fund of ways of telling the time of day or of naming the year without using numbers.

Our references are also not too specific. We say, "Somebody made a survey. . . ." We know that we should be precise in such things, but it is surprising how often we are not; deliberately, too, it seems.

Then there are words—a large group of them—that are not so specific as we seem to think they are.

Our instructions to audiences are not definite enough. We come to the end of the speech. We are assigning the task we want the group to do. And we don't state it specifically.

Let's talk about the way you express ideas. You say, "The package was damaged because of careless handling." That is a common statement, isn't it? But what happened? Did some fellow in the express company drop it? Was it thrown across a car by the friendly employee of the railroad? Was it mishandled in the mail? Did somebody lay a heavy crate on the "Fragile, Handle with Care" sticker? Was it dropped or bumped? Perhaps it makes no difference. But if it will help to tell what happened—if the audience should know—then tell them exactly what happened. That's what I mean by being specific. A man who introduces me many times says, "He is the author of many books on selling and sales management." That is true. But why didn't he name just one of the books? The mention might sell a copy or two. Strange how we dodge the specific.

Instead of saying that food budgets go further, why not tell what can be saved? Put it in dollars and cents if you can. Instead of speaking of the purity of soap, say that it is 99.44 per cent pure. One company has done that and is doing quite well.

Sometimes a speaker wants to include too much to be definite. Not long ago I looked over a script for a talk in which the man

used the term "service agencies." He was talking about various
kinds of business houses which service electric appliances. "Why
don't you say 'service shops'?" I asked him.

"I want it to cover everything," he replied. Now of course
there are a few companies servicing electric appliances that cannot be classified as service shops. And his service agencies did
cover everything. But if he had wanted to make himself clear he
would have done better to forget the larger field. He would have
done better if he tried to cover one pier rather than the whole
water front.

There is a lot of this kind of thinking in writing speeches. The
other day we were discussing what we would ask a group of salesmen to do in a speech we were writing. In the interest of making
the instructions specific, it was suggested: "Let's have each salesman ask for an order for three of the packages from every account." That seemed like a good idea, and the plan was adopted.

Then one of the group asked, "What will that do to the fellow
who would buy twelve?" Now there were a hundred who would
buy three for every five who would buy twelve, but the group
voted to cut out the mention of three. Instead, the talk would
ask the salesman to sell as many as possible. As a concession, after
much argument, the line read, "at least three to every account."
This latter statement was not so strong as the former, but it had
to do. Don't try to include everything. If you can leave out something and make the statement more specific, take the chance on
leaving out the extras.

Our tendency to add on illustrates this. We say "engineering,
manufacturing, and other such functions." Why not name those
other functions? So often the two named are all you need mention.
But adding "etc." has become a habit.

I have a friend who has developed the habit of saying "and so
forth and so on." In every talk he makes he uses that line a number
of times. The line means nothing. It adds nothing to his talk. I have
asked him about it and he says, "It's a peculiar habit, isn't it?
I suppose it is a sort of verbal recess until another thought strikes

me." If you have any verbal recesses, let's cut them out of your talk.

In the names of places and things we tend to steer away from the specific. We say, "I was walking down the street in a large Middle Western city." Why not say, "I was walking down Euclid Avenue in Cleveland"? We say, "I was sitting in the reception room in my favorite club." Why not name the club? The Elks, The K of C, the Eagles, the Moose, the Union League, or the Ajax Marching and Chowder. Such names are specific. They give the listener a better picture. They are a part of the lives of every one of us. Name the town, the street, the club, the hotel, the railroad. All of them are excellent speech material and they are better speech material when you are specific.

When you mention Euclid Avenue in Cleveland, the listener who knows that street gets a picture. If you say you were in the neighborhood of the Statler, he knows about where you were. Such references make a speech live. If you talk about a store, name the store. If you are talking about Cleveland, it is Higbee's, or May's, or Halle's, or Linder's. If you talk about a firm, name the firm. If you tell about a train trip you took, tell from where to where and name the railroad. Some of the listeners have made that trip too, and they will ride along with you. When you hear some speakers handle such material, you would think they were out for the FBI on a secret mission.

On dates we also are not so specific as we could be. Rule out all such expressions as "the turn of the century" or "in the early 1900's." It is just as easy to name the year—1899—1900—1901. You say, "A man in his middle fifties." Make him fifty-three or fifty-four. There is a bit more reality about the number.

If you are using data, check all your references and make them specific. Perhaps you have written "a recent survey." Change that to "a survey made by the National Association of Manufacturers in 1949." If you have said "reliable sources of information," change it to name the sources. Often when you use data from a survey, the group only half believes you anyway. They wonder how the survey was made. They question whether or not the survey people were hired to find out the truth or something that you wanted them to find out. Thus, when you quote a reference, be as specific as you can about it.

There is a long list of words used in speeches that should be checked. One that the men in the electrical business bandy about a lot is "automatic." We say an appliance is automatic when it adjusts itself, operates itself, does the work without attention, turns itself off and on. Here is what I mean.

A toaster is automatic when it adjusts its timing so that the toast is always the same, even though the toaster is cold for the first slice and hot on the tenth slice.

A washer is automatic when it takes the clothes through a cycle of washing, rinsing, and drying.

An electric iron is automatic when it turns itself on when current is needed to heat the iron to the temperature the user has selected, and turns itself off when the selected heat is reached.

An electric water heater is automatic when it turns on the electricity to heat the water when its temperature goes below the degree at which the thermostat is set, and turns itself off when the water is heated to the temperature setting of the thermostat.

All those appliances are automatic, yet if we are to be specific about them we can't use the one word "automatic" to describe them.

Another word we use a lot is "efficiency." We say that an appliance is efficient when we mean that it uses less electricity or costs less to operate. Not long ago I was talking to a man about an electric comforter. Because the comforter has a top layer of cotton batting over the warming sheet, the comforter is more efficient. It is more efficient because the heat is allowed to escape into the room more slowly. Because of that insulation on top, the warmth from the warming sheet stays in the bed. Now that makes the bed comforter more efficient, but it would be more specific to say that because of the insulation the heat does not escape into the room and so the comforter uses less electricity and costs less to operate. Those latter expressions are more specific. True, it is efficient, but when you say so you may not be telling the story you think you are telling.

The word "efficiency" is used in a number of such ways. If the appliance saves labor, it is efficient, or if it saves time or water or soap or cleaning. Those qualities make the appliance more efficient, but if the listener is to understand what you mean, you should say the appliance is efficient, and then tell why. The "why" helps make the statement specific.

"Economy" and "economical" are words in this class. A tire that runs 100,000 miles is more economical than one that runs 25,000 miles, but why not talk about that extra 75,000 miles? Often one word can't tell the story effectively.

"Ingredients" is another such word. We say, "Add the ingredients." It would be more specific if we named those ingredients. The home economist at the cooking school picks up the little roll of waxed paper and, holding it carefully, spills the contents into the bowl, where they are drawn into the whirling beaters of the mixer. She says, "I mixed these ingredients beforehand so as to save time here." I feel that it would be better for her to say, "The flour, salt, sugar, and baking powder are already mixed in this little roll of paper. I mixed them beforehand to save time here." This statement is more specific. Perhaps someone in the audience does not know what the ingredients are. It may be that they would like to know what ingredients can be mixed beforehand.

We use such expressions as "metal objects." In talking about a garbage disposer that fits into the sink, we say, "You can grind up anything but metal objects." We mean tin cans and bottle caps. We say the machine will grind all kitchen waste. We mean that it will grind all garbage. But even that is not enough. How about bones and olive pits? Do you get what I mean? "Metal objects" may mean tin cans and bottle caps to you. But it may mean automobile door handles, airplane wings, or hairpins to another. So if you are describing your product in your speech and telling what it will do, be specific.

The instructions you give should be checked. If you want your audience to do something, make your instructions specific. It is not enough to say, "Give to the Red Cross." It is much better to say, "Give more to the Red Cross this year than you did last year."

It is even better to say, "Give three dollars and fifty cents to the Red Cross."

Don't tell a group of salesmen to go and call on a large number of dealers. Tell them to call on every dealer they have. Tell them to call on three dealers a day. Cut into their understanding with a specific statement of what you want them to do.

Let's say your fund workers are assembled at a big breakfast. As soon as they finish that second cup of coffee they are to start calling on prospects. Don't tell them to call on all they can. Tell them to call on six today and six tomorrow. Don't tell them to use the literature to back up their sales talk. Explain how to use the literature, what to say, and what pictures to point out. Don't tell them to bring the pledge cards back to the office. Explain that they are to bring them to Miss Ajax, in room 212 on the second floor. So often in giving instructions in speeches we leave the listeners with a verbal wave of the hand. We can't do that. We must tell them exactly who, what, and how. Leave nothing to the imagination; don't expect them to figure out what to do. Tell them—specifically.

The law of averages can be a big help to you in being more specific. Let's say your speech tells a group of salesmen about a million-dollar magazine advertising campaign that your company is planning. You have written, "This campaign is costing the company a cool million dollars." That is a lot of money and, as such, it is impressive. But suppose these salesmen work in a territory that includes ten counties in one state. The million dollars isn't all being spent to help them. If there are 1,000 salesmen all over the country, that million dollars breaks down to one thousand dollars per salesman. When you tell me you are spending one thousand dollars to help me, you interest me. So why not say, "This campaign is costing the company a cool million dollars. Now how much is that for every one of you? It is one thousand dollars for each salesman —that's what it is. One thousand dollars for every salesman in the country—one thousand dollars for everyone in this room."

The amount every team should raise in a fund drive can be averaged out. Tell them that the total is $56,000. But then explain that, with twenty teams working, it amounts to $2,800 per team. Oh, I can hear some of you saying, "We can't do that, for some of the teams are expected to do more than others." That's right, they are. But if you can't be that specific, be as specific as you can. There are times when you can't use such averages, but when you can they are a big help.

In the advice we give in speeches we are often indefinite. We say, "Every young man should take a course in public speaking." It would be better if we said, "Every young man should take Dale Carnegie's course in public speaking." That advice would be better if we added some details about the course: where and when and how much. We say, "All of us should work on our vocabulary constantly." We may say, "Get a good book on vocabulary building—there are many of them." It would be much better if we named a book, told where it could be bought, and the price. So if you have any advice in your speech, check it again. Can you make it more specific?

I have evidence that listeners act on such advice. I did a talk in the Henry Grady Hotel in Atlanta, and after it a young man came up and said, "Mr. Hegarty, that book you referred to—is it called 'How to Run a Sales Meeting'?"

"It is," I admitted, beaming.

"Was this advice you just gave us in that book?" he asked.

"Every word of it and more," I agreed.

"Could you tell me where I might buy a copy?" he went on.

"There is a bookstore right next door," I said. "You might try there."

At the next intermission the young man was back to see me. "They had it," he said. He showed me the book, and I autographed it.

In that talk I had suggested that those who wanted to have better meetings should get the book. This fellow was interested and he acted on my advice. But I was specific. I said, "Buy my book." I named it and I probably quoted the price.

So try to make your speech specific. Look for such expressions as these: unprecedented situation, high official places, economic future, broad-gauge policies, potential obstacles, broader role, the broad selling argument, channels of consumption, major mechanical goods, economic dead center, sheer volume involved, mountainous amounts, major purchases, economic wheels turning, twofold responsibility, dominant position, at all levels, desirable ends, large segment of the nation. Yes, look for them, and when you find them, see if you can't substitute something more specific. I took all those expressions out of one speech. I believe that many of them can be improved—perhaps not all of them, but most.

Here, to sum up, are the suggestions covered:

1. Check your method of expressing ideas.
2. Use exact dates—not "the turn of the century."
3. Ditto for time—"it was two-thirty in the afternoon."
4. Name the places—the towns will like the advertising, and so will the hotels and the stores.
5. Be definite about your references. Tell who said it—not an eminent Scottish poet—it was Robert Burns, wasn't it?
6. Use words that have a definite meaning. You confuse me with words that can mean many things—efficiency, economy, automatic.
7. Expressions such as "metal objects" should be cleared up—they cover too broad a field—from watch springs to locomotives.
8. The additions—"this and that" and "things like that." The "things like that" should be named.
9. Check your instructions—are they specific?
10. Use the law of averages when you can to make the data apply more specifically to the listeners.
11. When you give advice give it specifically. Use names, dates, prices. They will be more likely to act if they know exactly what to do.

24. Shorten the Long Sentences

For the next check, consider the long sentences. Let's count the words between the periods and see what we can do about lessening the number. Why? Well, short sentences are easier to say. They allow you to put the emphasis where you want it. Here is an example.

"It is new, unique, ingenious, and different."

If I want to emphasize each of those four points, I could say:

"It is new. It is unique. It is ingenious. It is different."

Bang, bang, bang, bang—I can hit each word just as hard as I choose. It might be even more effective if I used a contraction of "it is," changing it to "it's." Then it would read:

"It's new. It's unique. It's ingenious. It's different."

The example is an exaggeration, but it explains the point.

When you talk in long sentences it is easy to get tangled up in something like this:

"These mounting, stormy tirades against American free enterprise during the last decade, far from wearing themselves out, have prospered and won new converts, because American management people have failed to provide the true story of the glorious achievements of American free industry."

Why is this true? Perhaps it is because too many management people speak in the language of this sentence. I'll bet the speaker who spoke that sentence was an orator. And that those inarticulate management people he mentions applauded his remark.

Some of this addiction to the long sentence may come from the newspaper reporter. He is taught to get enough into the first sentence so that a reader, caught by the headline, keeps on reading until he knows what the story is about. Here is an example:

> "Dedication of the new Wurlitzer electric organ purchased recently by the Grace Gospel Church will be held Sunday at 3 P.M., with Harold Byers, organist, presenting the program."

There are a number of ideas in that sentence. The church has a new organ. It is a Wurlitzer. It is electric. It will be dedicated Sunday at 3 P.M. Harold Byers, the organist, will present the program.

Suppose you were a member of the Men's Club of that church, and it was your job to tell the other members that the dedication was scheduled for Sunday and you wanted them all to attend. How would you say it? Surely not in the words of that lead sentence in the newspaper account. In speaking you do not have to get it all into the first sentence. Your audience is sitting there in front of you. They will continue sitting, and listening, you hope, while you say a number of sentences.

There are many reasons why the long sentence may get you into trouble. Here are a few:

1. You stumble over the wording.
2. You have a tendency to use meaningless phrases.
3. You lose a portion of the idea.
4. You make yourself more difficult to understand.
5. You so load the sentence with ideas that you lose emphasis on any one of them.
6. You ask the audience to make too much effort to understand you.

A long sentence is difficult to speak. Pick up any magazine and select a ten-word sentence. Read it as if you felt strongly about the idea expressed. You are fighting madly for this cause, or you are howling against it. Give the sentence reading your all. Now try a twenty-word sentence. Read it aloud. Try to put the same force, the same conviction into the reading. I am sure that the demonstration will explain what I mean.

"But," you say, "in the movies and on the stage the actors use long sentences." That's true, they do. But those sentences are rehearsed. In the movies they photograph and record one short scene at a time, but before the scene is taken the lines are gone over again and again. They are carefully timed and punctuated with gestures and facial expressions. Each scene is photographed a number of times and only the best of the shots is used.

In a stage play they say the same lines night after night. Yet even so, some long-run plays are rehearsed two or three times a week. Stage managers know that for long speeches to be right they must be rehearsed.

Your speech will probably be made only once. True, you'll rehearse it some. But you won't go over the wording again and again to make sure that your delivery is perfect. Therefore, cut out those long sentences because the short ones are easier to say.

I can't explain why speakers use such long sentences. Yet they do. A short time ago I heard a speaker say:

"It is a perfectly normal and proper question to ask whether this tendency is temporary." Try saying that.

Now, try saying this:

"Far be it from me to resort to the statistics of the economist for proof of the fact that the years ahead offer American industry a golden opportunity to prove its soundness and ability." Difficult, isn't it?

That sentence is long. It is also loaded with meaningless words. The speaker could have said, "The years ahead offer American industry a golden opportunity to prove its soundness and ability." That "Far be it from me . . ." phrase is not needed. We often pad our "prepared remarks" with such meaningless phrases. A long sentence permits these to creep in. So let's check over the script looking for periods. If we find them spaced too far apart, let's put them closer together.

One reason for the short sentence is that when you try to speak the long one you lose a portion of the idea. Remember my point about the adjectives. If you use an adjective that is too strong, you lose the noun it was supposed to modify. If you use a weak ad-

jective, you lose the adjective. It is tough, but you can't win. Here
is a long sentence that illustrates that point:

> Charts can be used to list facts and statistical data which the audi-
> ence can grasp at a glance, and then retain as a vivid mental impres-
> sion.

When that sentence is spoken, the comma gives it the effect of
two sentences. But in the writing, the speaker might just as well
have made that clause after the comma a separate sentence. If I were
writing that sentence for speaking, it would go:

> Charts can be used to list facts and statistical data. (First idea)
> The audience grasps the facts and the data at one glance. (Second
> idea) It retains them as a vivid mental impression. (Third idea)

That is better, but the material should be worked over again to
make it speak easier. Just say those three sentences aloud. They
don't speak too well, do they? Let's try again.

> Charts can be used to list facts and statistical data. The speaker
> turns the chart. The audience sees the data. It reads and grasps the
> message. And it retains that message as a vivid mental impression.

That is better as speaking material. There are ten more words in
this version than the original. Now let's see what happens when
the adjectives are discarded. The passage will then read:

> Charts can be used to list data. The speaker turns the chart. The
> audience sees the data. It grasps the message. It retains it. Why? Be-
> cause by using a chart, the speaker has given a second impression.
> This impression is more likely to be remembered.

There are almost twice as many words in this example as in the
original, but this passage will speak well. Try it aloud. The complete idea is expressed in the first five sentences. Here:

> Charts can be used to list data. The speaker turns the chart. The
> audience sees the data. It grasps the message. It retains it.

Those twenty-five words express the three ideas in the original passage. In my talk called "How to Make a Chart Talk" I make two of the points in these words:

> Charts give a second impression. They give you something to look at. The picture emphasizes what I say. It helps you remember.

That has one more word than the passage that started this discussion. Perhaps it doesn't express the same ideas, but it comes close. And it will speak. I know for I have spoken it before audiences.

The long sentence can be difficult to understand. Not long ago I heard a man discuss the recruiting of college men. The following is one of the sentences he used. It seemed unusually long as he said it, and I got this transcript from the stenotypist.

> A number of companies have empowered their personnel men to make job offers on the college campuses at the time of the interview or to make the job offer by mail without offering to the applicant the opportunity to visit and talk to the sales executives of the company.

There are forty-nine words in that sentence. It is long. And it is difficult to ferret out the meaning. You know as you read it that the speaker thought of that speech as "my prepared address." Let's break that sentence up into the thoughts expressed.

> Some personnel men make job offers on the college campuses. They are empowered to do this at the time of the interview. Or they make the job offer by mail. The applicant gets no opportunity to visit the factory and talk to the sales executives.

Of course, this passage could be made better for speaking if it was entirely rewritten. You may say, "The fellow read that speech." That's right, he did. If he had read the sentence as a number of short ones, it would have sounded better. It would be better for speaking if it were written:

> Some personnel men make job offers on the college campuses. Some make offers by mail. In either case, the applicant does not have the opportunity to visit the factory and talk to the sales executives.

This last is better. Try reading that first passage aloud. You are trying to make the point that the young man from the college should be allowed to visit the factory and talk to the sales executives. You feel strongly about this point. So put some force into the reading. Give it all you've got.

Next try reading that first revision. It goes better, doesn't it? Now try the second revision. Do you see what those long sentences do to the force that you can put into a speech?

Sam Vining says that he doesn't worry too much about the length of the sentences in a script he speaks. He says, "I can put in the periods by a shrug of my shoulders, or a wave of my hands." He can, too—and make the audience like it. But there are only a few Sam Vinings in this country. So, get those periods spaced closer together.

One of the difficulties of the long sentence is that you may lose the emphasis. How would you put emphasis on any one of the ideas listed in this sentence?

> The general pressure for full employment and the desire of business in its own interest to provide for employment leads to only one conclusion, namely, that volume consumption is necessary in order to provide markets, and that high employment becomes impossible without consumption at a rate greater than ever before.

It would take a skillful speaker to use that sentence and not lose his audience along the way. He would need all the tricks—gestures, pauses, changes in his manner of speaking, perhaps even a bit of silence. But the sentence can be broken up into short sentences. One way to look at this job of working on the long sentences is to think about how that kind of sentence would break up in a conversation between two businessmen. Let's see how it looks that way:

> "The country needs full employment."
> "Yeah, and business needs it too. How can business make a profit with a lot of unemployed?"
> "It can't—so we've got to sell everything the factories can make."

"And the factories are bigger, so we've got to sell more than we ever did before."

Conversation always does that to ideas. For in conversation you pause, and you repeat, and you emphasize, and you put in those connectives that make the difference. Conversation has life. It is easier to listen to, it is easier to read.

In making these revisions, don't leave out any ideas that you feel are important. Don't change the ideas. Just change the way you express them so that the audience has a better chance to understand.

Let's consider that sentence that I quoted above. It is out of the proceedings of a sales conference. About five hundred men paid ten dollars to get into that conference. They came to learn. They were serious about it. They needed ideas. Now most of those men would attempt to listen to the speaker. But because of the way he tried to load all his ideas into one sentence, they would have to listen intently.

I admit that the speaker did not get paid for his effort, and you may ask, "Why should he try to make it clearer? If the dummies can't understand that, it is their funeral."

That is right, it is. But if the speaker is trying to persuade the audience to do something, he should try to make himself clear. And he should try to make it easier for the audience to listen. If you use long, involved sentences, the audience will have to listen intently to get your meaning. If you use short sentences—one idea per sentence—it does not have to listen so intently. Which kind of talk would you rather hear?

Politicians and statesmen resort to the long sentence. Here is a gem culled from one of the Washington columns:

> Our government could not possibly expect to find the necessary support for a policy involving military alliance with a power that continues to lend sanction, tacit or active, to evils of the very kind which it is the objective of the proposed pact to oppose and prevent.

That is a lulu. I challenge you to write it in any form that is easier to speak. Take five minutes by your watch and try to unscramble it. Chances are you will give up, saying, "Let's start all over."

It seems that the learned gentleman is trying to say:

> Our people would never go for supporting one gang of cutthroats against another gang of cutthroats.

Any speaker using such long sentences might easily stumble over the wording. The idea expressed in the following sentence is clear enough, but just try saying it:

> "Retail selling has deteriorated to a level where its identity with basic, constructive salesmanship is virtually lost."

That seems to be going a long way around to say:

> "Retail selling just ain't selling."

As you start revising your long sentences, you will cut words and you will add words. We are considering here how sentences sound when they are spoken, not how well or how poorly they are written in your script.

Rudolf Flesch in his book *The Art of Plain Talk* * gives a table which shows how the length of sentences affects the ease of reading. Here it is:

AVERAGE SENTENCE LENGTH IN WORDS

Very easy	8 or less
Easy	11
Fairly easy	14
Standard	17
Fairly difficult	21
Difficult	25
Very difficult	29 or more

These numbers refer to the average length of sentences. The "easy" piece may have some eight-word sentences, and some four-

---

* From *The Art of Plain Talk* by Rudolf Flesch. New York, Harper & Brothers, 1946. Copyright 1946 by Rudolf Flesch.

teen, but the average length is eleven words. I am not certain that these lengths apply exactly to the spoken sentence but they give you an idea. When you write a sentence you should be allowed to use more words because the reader sees the sentence and so has a chance to study it. Where you speak a sentence he can't stop to study it, for you are going on. There is another difference. When you speak you can use the speaker's tricks of gesture, inflection, emphasis, pause. The table, then, is presented as a reference. If you are interested in plain talk, get Dr. Flesch's book and study it. It is interesting, easy to read, and will give you ideas on how to express your ideas simply and effectively.

Perhaps you have written no long sentences in your speech. But check to see. It is an easy check to make. Scan the speech. When you come to a sentence that looks long, check it. If you can break it up into two or more short sentences, do so.

By handling the clauses of a long sentence as separate sentences you can get the effect of a number of short sentences strung together. In speaking of the uses of advertising as a help in war activities, a speaker said:

> Words in print. Words to sell products. To sell war bonds. To recruit Wacs, Waves, Spars. To salvage paper, tin, fats. To get blood donors. To do a hundred-and-one jobs.

Try speaking that aloud. It goes well, doesn't it? You may say, "But with short sentences like that you sound like the rat-tat-tat of a machine gun." That is right, you do. My suggestion is that you cut the exceptionally long sentences into shorter ones. But don't have all short sentences. Use a ten-word, then a five-word, then a seven-word sentence. Mix them up. Put three or four short sentences together if you want the effect of bang, bang, bang. But for the best effect throughout the talk, mix the lengths.

In suggesting that you cut down the long sentences, I am not suggesting that you cut out ideas. No, leave them in, but don't load them all in one poor sentence. The sentence creaks at the joints and some of your meaning leaks out. Here is a summary of the suggestions:

1. Count the words between periods. If you have over ten, check to see why.
2. If the long sentence has more than one idea, can you give each idea a sentence of its own?
3. Are the meaningless phrases necessary? Do they add the color you feel you need? Do they get in the way of the meaning?
4. Is the idea expressed clearly? Read the sentence to the ever-loving wife and ask her to tell you what you meant. Remember she has been confused by what you said before.
5. Is all of the idea clear? Is each part clear?
6. How about emphasis? What do you want to emphasize about this idea? Can you do it with the sentence length as is?
7. Can you say the sentence aloud without stumbling over the wording? Try it. Then try saying it as two sentences.
8. If the audience has to listen intently to get the idea, they won't like it. Will they have to listen intently to get the meaning of this sentence?
9. Have you varied the length of the sentences throughout the script?
10. Count the number of words in all the sentences in the script and average them out. How does the average compare with the Rudolf Flesch table on page 178?
11. Remember that you can punctuate the long sentences by such speaking tricks as gestures, shrugs of the shoulders, and pauses. If you plan to use such devices, write them into the script, and practice doing them.

Now that we have cleared up the long sentences, let's get on with a discussion of the next check.

25. Trim the Wordage

In making this check you will have fun. And you will learn a lot too. You're not given to excess wordage, are you? You don't think so. But wait until you get through this check. Montesquieu said, "What orators want in depth, they make up for in length." While you are not trying to be an orator, I hope you can still do a lot of cutting with profit if your speech is written like most speeches. Almost anything can be written shorter. Perhaps in this speech you do not have a gem like that used by the fight announcer as the battle for the heavyweight title started. He said, "May the crown of victory descend on the brow of the more worthy participant." That is putting "May the best man win" in a full quota of words. But don't laugh—we all do it. Perhaps you have a number of such passages in your speech. The average speech writer adds words to his script in a number of ways. Here are a few:

1. The way you say things—most of us are wasteful of words.
2. The sayings that make you sound like a stuffed shirt.
3. Saying the same thing twice and not for repetition or emphasis.
4. The use of two words where one will do.
5. The introductions to ideas that don't help express the ideas.
6. The extra lines in the anecdotes.
7. The additions, the etcs. You keep on talking after you stop.
8. The adjectives—the ones that don't register.
9. The mentions of time.
10. The connectives.

Let's talk first about the way you throw words around. I have to assume that you do this, because almost everybody else does. For instance, you mention your speech. "In this speech I am going to give tonight. . . ." Why shouldn't that be:

"In my speech tonight . . ."? If you have written: "In my talk I am going to do. . . ." change it to:

"In my talk. . . ." Not long ago I heard a speaker say: "I am in the process of reading a book." That could well be: "I am reading a book."

We use a lot of this kind of language in business. We say: "This knob enables you to turn the radio on and off."

There are a large number of words that are used in the way "enables" is used in the line above: "This knob allows. . . ." "This knob permits. . . ."

Very often the statement is stronger when it is made directly. Let the knob do the job directly and you save words. In writing a letter, or a description of a machine, we will quite likely write, "This knob permits. . . ." And so when we write a speech, we might use the same wording. But if you are trying to cut words, a word here and a word there adds up.

Speeches seem to be filled with expressions such as: "To get this job of training retail salesmen done." "He would be a good friend to have." "Advise a young man what to do to succeed."

Each of those might be written in less words. Thus: "To train retail salesmen." "He would make a good friend." "Advise a young man how to succeed."

Save a word here and there and you tighten up the speech. Not long ago, a man complained to me that he did not have enough time on the program to tell his story properly. "They gave me ten minutes and my script runs twelve," he said.

"Do you have your script written?" I asked.

He produced it and we went over it. By trimming excess wordage we got it down to the time limit. When he made the speech he finished in nine minutes. After it was over, he admitted, "That trimming made the speech better. The audience liked it."

Most audiences will like the speech that is direct and to the point. That excess wordage consumes time, and that time belongs to the audience. Frequently extra wordage doesn't help, and if it doesn't help it should be left out.

At times every speaker sounds like a stuffed shirt. Almost always it is because of words and phrases that he might just as well have omitted. A speaker says:

"It is axiomatic that individual effort can produce effective results only if the worker is satisfactorily motivated."

The speaker who mouths a line like that must be a stuffed shirt. The wording is beautiful. Even I admit that. But it doesn't go well in a speech. I know, because I listened to it. The same thought could be expressed simply: "A man works only when he has the urge to work."

I have taken down many lines such as this: "The next step is to find out the fundamental reasons and to take steps to correct those reasons."

That is not so bad as the other, but it can be simplified: "The next step is to find out why and to do something about it."

You may shed large, salty tears when you change such expressions as: "In the forefront of so many phases of human activity" to—"Up to his neck in everything." Or—

"From a condition of chronic financial illness to one of abundant prosperity" to—"From loss to profit." Or— "From red to black."

Yes, you may shed large, salty tears, but you will help the speech. And the audience will think of you as a regular Joe, the kind of fellow it likes to do business with.

Just the other day one of my friends said in a speech: "the securement of adequate consumption."

This fellow is regular—there is nothing of the stuffed shirt about him—until he gets up to make a speech. Then he lets himself go with material like that quoted above. In that line, a change of one word would have made the difference. There is nothing wrong with "adequate consumption." It is that word "securement" that doesn't belong. Change that to "getting" and the line can be spoken by anybody.

Usually when you stop to analyze the wording of a phrase that sounds "stuffed-shirtish" you find that it doesn't take much revision to put it in words that any simple person can speak. Here is a lead line in a talk that illustrates that point:

> "With the scarcity of products we have experienced in the past eight years most retailers have had little trouble in disposing of the domestic appliances that were available to them."

Change three or four words in that passage and it would speak better. Let's try this:

> "With the shortage of products in the past eight years, most retailers have had little trouble in selling any home appliance they could get."

The revision changes four words and leaves another one out. But it is now in words that anyone can speak. So check the words you have used—do they make you sound like a stuffed shirt?

Next, how many times have you said the same thing twice? You may have done it in words of slightly different meanings, but are those exact meanings apparent to the audience? Here is the kind of doubles I mean:

cooperation and coordination	efficiency and effectiveness
adequately and effectively	good and sufficient
authenticity and validity	ranting and raving
kith and kin	snare and delusion

fictitious or otherwise

At times these doubles become triples. Here are two:

Freely, frankly, and fearlessly
Illuminating, dramatic, and conclusive

Many doubles and triples crop up in speeches. Sometimes that second word helps, but often it doesn't. Go through the script and look them over. If they help, leave them in. If not, give them the blue pencil.

Here is another way of saying things twice. You hear speakers say: "trained technicians," "creative imagination," "skilled research men."

Aren't all technicians trained? Isn't all imagination creative? Aren't all research men more or less skilled? I mention these examples to the speaker who had used two of them in one session. I asked him if he thought the two words were needed. He said, "There is a redundancy there." I looked up "redundancy" in the dictionary. The definition was "superfluity, excess." That is what I mean. Such doubles are a habit with the man who uses them. Whenever he writes the word "technician" he puts the adjective "trained" before it. That is how he thinks of technicians. Then too, a technician sounds more important when you say he is "trained." But we are discussing trimming the wordage in your speech. This is another way to cut words and save time.

In our introductions to ideas we use many excess words. Not long ago I heard a speaker say:

> With all sincerity and without fear of contradiction, I can say that this new advertising campaign gives us more coverage than any previous campaign.

He could have expressed the same idea by saying:

> This advertising gives us more coverage than any previous campaign.

Perhaps the worst of this sort of thing is the speaker who starts:

> It is highly gratifying that so many of you have taken advantage of the opportunity to come to this meeting tonight.

To hear you talk, you mean? It sounds pretty, doesn't it? But I'm sure that the same thought can be expressed in less words.

Perhaps you need an introduction to your idea. You may need some words to tie the new idea into what has gone before. If so, try to make that transition as brief as possible. Few of the introductions you use will be as wordy as the one above, but most of us have a whole repertory of these connectives. Most of them are habit, too. Here are a few that I have written down as speakers said them:

in this case	let us say
as a matter of fact	shall we call it
generally speaking	now the question is
in general	incidentally
it so happens	far be it from me
the fact of the matter is	to begin with
at the other end of the scale	lest you think this too pessimistic
on the other hand	it behooves us
in fact	in other words
by the same token	to summarize
you may not believe this	basically
conversely	according to the best studies
in my own individual case	from a recent study

under these conditions

Now many of those terms are useful to the speaker. Others could be eliminated with benefit to the speech. I am not suggesting that you cut out all such connectives, but I suggest that you check each one. If it helps, leave it stand.

Many of the lines in our anecdotes can be eliminated. We say such things as:

to insert a slightly humorous note
I can't resist reporting an incident
I am reminded of the story
whereupon he replied
asseverated the judge
recently remarked to me
couched in language of the gutter

Each time you hear an anecdote you are quite likely to hear some such excess language as that above. Most of it is unnecessary. The anecdote can start without introduction. If you are using it to make a point, begin the story at the start without any apology or explanation. This will save wordage.

Words you added on can in many cases be cut out. In Chap. 23 I talked about those "and so forths" that were not specific. Now let's look at all the additions, specific or not. Let's see if they are needed. Here are some of the type phrases I mean:

in any way, shape or form
if you please
or for any other reason
the campaign details, including advertising and promotion
or anything else for that matter
as the case may be
if you will

Check over all the "and so forths" in your script, and see how many of them you can eliminate without taking away from your meaning.

Adjectives offer a big opportunity for this type of editing. Too often it is the writer in you puts them in the script. Check every adjective to see if it is needed, and I would suggest that you cut out every double. Here are some to illustrate:

two-way stretch   high-priority order
semiconscious observer   ever-growing menace
double-edged deal   drawn-steel construction
outmoded system   tri-snap thermostat
heart-warming instances   twofold job
grease-laden dirt   five-point success story
                semidarkened room

The double adjective comes from the writer's desire to crowd all the meaning he can into a few words. But the double adjective does not speak well. I have heard men say "drawn steel" when describing a product and I could not understand them. A speech is spoken to be understood, and if the listener does not hear the adjective, it might as well be left out.

You may ask, "But how about these radio announcers and their adjectives?" You have me there. The boys doing the commercials surely give with the adjectives. But remember those commercials are rehearsed. The announcer goes over them again and again. He works on his timing, volume, pitch, and inflection, as well as his voice quality. Even then he sometimes stumbles. I think the radio commercials overwork the adjectives, and I would suggest that you use them sparingly.

You might try your voice on these that I took from speeches:

singular honor	pithy story
vital point	feigned amazement
immediate copy	irrepressible reporter
dangerous parallel	material substance
individual initiative	altruistic member
eloquent effusion	efficacious measures
native wit	prime consideration

sporadic effort

As you look over that list you will find adjectives that express an idea that could not be so well expressed in a number of words. Adjectives do that. They condense a highly involved thought into a single word. But in speaking the adjective with the noun you may lose one word or the other.

There are many adjectives that sound all right—even in the examples given. This is perhaps because they are familiar to you. Saying "tri-snap thermostat" to an audience that knew thermostats might cause no misunderstanding but the same term to a popular audience might mean nothing. Check all adjectives. They offer a field for elimination.

We come now to the mentions of time. All are useless. The time you are mentioning belongs to the audience. Get that point, please. You say, "In the time at my disposal. . . ." Whose time—theirs, isn't it? None of these mentions of time helps. And there are so many of them!

I'm not going to be long on this
to tell it briefly
because of the brevity of time
we have a busy afternoon
I could go on for a long time
I don't have time to cover this thoroughly
this can't be told in ten minutes
here is a quick explanation
briefly, this is it

Cut all of these time mentions, for the audience is tickled pink when they get a quick explanation, or when you save their time by doing a twenty-minute speech in ten.

Another field for cutting are those phrases which bring in your own wishes. Such things as:

I'd like to take this opportunity
If I may be permitted to say
I'd like to tell you
I want to say one more little thing
I'd like to present to you
Let me summarize
Allow me to emphasize
If I may generalize
Let me repeat
May I suggest in passing
I, personally, want to

Why not say it, tell them, present it, repeat it, or make the suggestion without asking permission? The request for permission uses words, and words are time.

A word here and a word there makes a difference in the speaking time, but more difference in the quality of the speech. So let's get after excess wordage. Let's try to cut without taking away from the meaning or without losing color. But let's cut. Don't think that you are unusual because you find a lot to cut out. Not long ago an associate looked over my shoulder at a speech I was revising. "Did you write that originally?" he asked, when he saw the pencil marks on the typewritten copy.

I admitted that I did.

"You're sure tough on your own stuff," he said.

Perhaps so, and you should be tough on your stuff too.

Here is a review of the suggestions for cutting:

1. Check for your use of excess words—don't use ten words where one will do.
2. Cut out all expressions that make you sound like a stuffed

shirt. "With your kind permission I will depart from my prepared remarks."

3. Cut out those words that say the same thing twice: "authenticity and validity."

4. Check for those places where you have said the same thing twice without getting the emphasis or repetition that you should: "trained technicians."

5. Look over all introductions to ideas. Are they needed in this case to help your talk? This is one place where we seem to go overboard in the use of words.

6. Cut the overwordage out of the anecdotes you tell. In speaking a story you must use more words than in a written version. But use the right kind of words.

7. Cut all "and so forths" that are not helpful.

8. Look over all adjectives carefully. Do they help, and will you be able to pronounce them so that the audience will hear what you say? Cut all double adjectives—most speakers run the two words together.

9. Mention of time is no help at all. Cut all of them. A speaker should never mention time in his talk.

10. Check carefully for all excess words. If you need them for color or timing or emphasis, leave them in. But if they can be cut, out with them.

26. Let's Check the Big Words

Seven-letter, eight-letter, nine-letter, ten-letter, yes sir, these are the words you want to cut out. Anything you can say in the five-dollar word can be said just as well and perhaps more clearly in a number of smaller words.

When we write a speech we are much like the farmer's boy. When the father was asked if a year in college had made any difference in his eldest son, he replied, "Well, he is still a good hand with the plow, but I notice his language has changed some. It used to be, 'Whoa, Becky, haw, and git up.' Now when he comes to the end of the row he says, 'Halt, Rebecca, pivot, and proceed.' I'm not sure that Becky understands."

The big words are always good for a laugh. Joe, the boy in the next office says, "This epitomizes. . . ." Before he has finished the sentence, the boys are off with the razzberry. For Joe isn't that kind of fellow. And his use of the big word seems an affectation.

You may know the big words. You may know each and every one of them. But your audience—does it know them? When you say the big word, one member of the audience turns to his neighbor and asks, "What did he say?" The neighbor shakes his head, "I don't know."

Last week at a meeting in Buffalo, I asked the man next to me, "What did he say?"

The fellow replied, "I didn't hear it."

"Then why are you laughing?" I asked.

"It must have been funny," he said. "Everybody else is laughing."

That's the trouble with audiences. They don't tell you that they don't hear you or don't understand. They sit there acting as if they do. And that is why you want to make it as easy as possible for them to understand your speech.

What manner of words are we after on this check?

1. The long words, the words with seven or more letters. They stand out in the manuscript and are easiest to spot.
2. The unusual words, those words we know, and perhaps use every day, but that can be improved.
3. The common but difficult to say.
4. The hyphenated words.
5. The familiar but stiff words that can be changed into ones that are simpler or easier to say.
6. The manufactured words.
7. The long adjectives.
8. The "verys." Let's cut all of them out.

Please remember, I do not claim to be an expert on words, but I do claim to be an expert on speeches. An expert listener, anyway. The suggestions I make here come from my notes. As I sit in meetings listening I make notes of the words that don't sound well in speeches. The speaker cannot say them nearly so well as he could a few simpler words that would express the same meaning. I make it a point when I am making my talk "How to Run a Sales Meeting" at a business conference to list the big words that other speakers use. Then in my talk I tell the audience of the number of such words that were used so far that day. Here is a list that I took down in one meeting:

insatiable	purification	appalling
ecstasies	implementing	placating
rehabilitated	immemorial	temerity
peroration	precarious	dispersion
meticulous	specious	respondent
connotation	enunciated	utilization
motivation	dipsomaniac	competency
participate	sporadic	generic
legion	prerequisites	

Speakers at business meetings frequently read their speeches, and a speech that is written will contain such words. Even so, they don't read aloud well. It makes no difference whether the man is reading or speaking. Let's see what can be done with the words on that list—what words can be substituted:

insatiable	can't be satisfied	specious	plausible
purification ...	cleaning	respondent	the other guy
appalling	shocking	connotation	meaning
ecstasies	joys	enunciated	said
implementing ..	supporting	utilization	use
placating	satisfying	motivation	urge
rehabilitated ...	restored	dipsomaniac ...	drunk
immemorial ...	long ago	competency ...	ability
temerity	foolhardiness	participate	take part
peroration	wind up, finish	sporadic	single
precarious	uncertain	generic	of a kind
dispersion	scattering	legion	a great number
meticulous	careful	prerequisite	requirement

Those words I have substituted may not be exact synonyms for the words spoken. But as I wrote down the words, I wrote beside it a word that would have brought out the meaning. On some of these words my choice was little better than the speaker's but there are some thoughts and ideas that can't be expressed in small simple words.

Not long ago in looking over a script for a movie the following words were cut out of the narrator's talk. Each was replaced by two or more words that had the same meaning and were much simpler.

placement	constitute	preventing	permanent
facilities	utilize	functional	transition
visualize	intrigues	persuading	unappreciative
advising	consult	source	reveals
structural	alternation	acquired	obstruction

Try your hand at substituting simpler words for the words on that list. You will find the exercise interesting and stimulating.

In working with narrators who make the sound tracks for films, I have found that the words they stumble over are words like those listed. Give these professional men short, simple words to say and they will record a script perfectly, and although they can handle involved words too, they are more likely to make slips. When the announcer stumbles on a recording, the record has to be accepted with the mistake, or it has to be cut over. For that reason a script that has few involved words can save everybody's time.

Probably the best way to illustrate what the elimination of the large words means is to do some eliminating. Here is a paragraph from a speech I heard.

> The impact of the phrase "postwar planning" on the consciousness of the marketing executive will not solely be a measure of his optimism, but perhaps of his foresight as well.

Let's cut all the words that have seven or more letters. The passage would then read:

> The impact of that phrase—postwar planning—on the sales manager will be a measure of his optimism and perhaps of his foresight as well.

We are still stuck with three words that are longer than seven letters. Let's see what we can do about them:

> The impact of that phrase—plans for postwar—on the sales manager will be a measure of his faith and of his ability to look ahead.

Now the passage is down in shorter words. I don't claim too much for it, but it illustrates my point, and it will speak better.

Here is another that we might work on:

> Our purpose is to build a sales program that will sell through the channel of distribution a sufficient quantity of merchandise to provide continuous production and continuous employment for the majority of American workers.

As you look over that passage you find no unusual words. But let's cut out the seven-letter words:

Our purpose is to build a sales program that will sell through the stores enough goods to keep both the factory and the workers on the job five days per week.

That is taking some liberty with the passage, but it is a liberty that is based on knowledge of what the speaker meant. His channel of distribution was retail stores. His full employment meant a forty-hour week.

Such a revision can be made on most such passages. That one would have meant the same if it were written thus:

Our objective is a sales program that will keep the factory working five days per week.

Let's analyze that. If the factory works, the workers work. In working on the big words, the passage has been cut in length. It is down to fifteen words now, and the original passage had thirty-three. As you study your script you will find that eliminating the big words may help you cut the number of words.

There are times, of course, when the big word is the only one that will express the thought you want to get over. The other day in checking a script for a meeting we were eliminating big words and substituting smaller ones. Somewhere in the discussion my associates said that the script lacked something. "Yes, it lacks spontaneity," I said.

He laughed and said, "But we are getting rid of the big words."

I could have said that the script lacked life and laughter and sparkle. It did lack all those. But when stuck for a word I came up with one of eleven letters. My line would have been much better speech material if I had said, "It lacks life and laughter and sparkle." My diagnosis would have been more nearly correct too. I am not suggesting the elimination of the big word because of meaning. Many times the big word will express the meaning better. I suggest that the big words be dropped because the small words speak better.

The other night on the radio the hard-boiled father of the girl said he was going to the dentist. "I have a tooth that hurts terrible," he said.

"Are you going to have it extracted?" asked the young swain who was courting the daughter.

"Naw, I'm goin' to have it pulled," the father said.

It is that type of clarity you want in your speech, and short words will help give it to you.

Let's check too for the familiar words that can be changed to ones that sound better in speeches. I've written a book called *How to Run a Meeting*. Time and time again when I'm introduced as a speaker, the chairman says, "Mr. Hegarty has written several books, among them one called *How to Conduct a Meeting*. To me there is a lot of difference in those words. I feel that a meeting that is "conducted" is rather stiff and formal. One that's run might have some life in it. There are many such words. When I talk about eliminating them and substituting simpler ones, I buy myself a lot of arguments. There is nothing wrong with the words themselves for they express the speaker's meaning; even so, the simpler, more common word makes better speech material.

Here are some of these words and suggested substitutions:

accompany	go with	remote	far away
accomplished	did	removes	takes out, or off
admits	says	replace	put back
affirms	says	reprimand	bawl out
appreciable	many	required	needed
arrival	coming	resolve	decide
avails	profits	respond	answer
ascertain	find out	return	come back
assists	helps	retort	answer
available	can be had	revise	change
awaiting	waiting for		
receives	gets	seeking	looking for
refrain	hold back	similar	same kind
recently	not long ago	surmises	guesses
recognize	know	utilize	use

There is another kind of word that speakers like to use. It is what I call "the unusual"—words that are not heard often enough for listeners to grasp quickly. Here is a list taken from speeches, with words that might be substituted:

harbored	....	held (idea)	naïveté	......	simplicity
pragmatic	...	practical	specious	.....	plausible
surmised	.....	guessed	impels	....	forces
impinges	.....	bumps	macabre	.....	gruesome
persists	......	continues	of that era	...	of that time
		aggregate	....	total	

The trouble with the words in this list is that the audience may know them casually, but may not be too familiar with their usage. You say the word "specious." I know what the word means, but the meaning doesn't immediately come to me. And so I stop to think. I don't have time for that in listening to a speech. You say "plausible" and I get it faster. You say "sounds like the truth—but isn't" and I have no doubt. Get the idea?

As you study the words in this list you see that some substitutes are almost as unusual as the originals. You may question some of the synonyms, but they give more quickly the meaning the speaker meant to convey. There is nothing wrong with the words used. They probably express exactly what the writer meant. But note that I said "writer."

Let's check out the manufactured words. The other night I heard a speaker say "re-lamping." He was describing a lighting fixture and the ease of putting a lamp in it. To an audience of men in his business, the expression would have been easily understood. But this was a popular audience made up of members of a service club and their wives. Check all such words.

Occasionally, when you have to use such a word, you might take the time to explain it. If you don't you may have difficulty making the audience understand. You might say the manufactured word, then spell it out. The explanation will be clearer if you hold up a card with the words printed on it. You should take the trouble to make sure that your audience understands.

There is a great deal of this type of wording in business talks that describe product or plans. Where the name of a special feature is new, use some method to help the audience understand. If the plan or policy has a new name, make sure that the name is understood when you mention it.

I have given some attention to adjectives before, but I would like to put in another word about them. This time I want to mention the seven-letter ones, such as:

primary	first	specialized ...	special
cardinal	top	radical	different
inferior	not so good	essential	necessary
consistent	steady	apathetic	not interested

The first two in the list are used with "objective" in the speech notes I have taken. Wouldn't it be just as well to say, "our first objective" or "our number one objective," or "our top objective"? Usually these adjectives can be changed and the passage given more force.

I'd suggest that you cut out every "very." That word, too, is much of a habit. A long time ago I read that bit of advice in a piece by Alexander Woollcott. Since then I have been trimming the "verys" out of my scripts. It's strange, but the line always seems better without it.

There is another group of words that finds favor with speakers. These words end with "able." Here are some that I noted in speeches:

sizeable amount	why not large?
easily obtainable	easy to get
readily conceivable	anyone could imagine
inescapable fact	we don't run from facts, or do we?
enviable position	the top, or wherever it is
foreseeable	not too far off

Now I am going to break your heart. I ask that you cut out all those passages that you put in the script to show your brilliance in the expression of ideas. Let's check them with the eyes of the other fellow. Perhaps you have written some such drivel as "heart-warming instances of gracious contact with buyers," or "success-fully able to override his objections." Look at those two expres-sions and you can see what you must do with them. They are beautiful, but a little on the dumb side. And you don't want your audience to think you are dumb.

That gives you some idea of the kind of words that make bet-ter speeches—the smaller and simpler the words, the better the speech material. Let's go over the suggestions again:

1. Try to eliminate the long words. Perhaps you know what they mean. But they may not be understood.
2. Let's check on the unusual words. Do you always remember what "unctious" means?
3. Then take care of the known but stiff words. Don't "re-move" your coat—"take it off."
4. Let's dispense with the hyphenated words. Make that "wind-blown hair" either "mussed" or something that the audience can understand when you pronounce it.
5. Change those familiar but stiff words into simpler words that are easier to say. "Do" things instead of "accomplishing" them.
6. Do what you can to make any manufactured words clear, even if you have to spell them out on a card or blackboard.
7. Watch those long adjectives. Those "essential" words are not so essential.
8. Cut out every "very." You will find they don't help anyway.
9. Check out most of the words that end in "able." There is usually a word that is not so stiff that will give you the same meaning.

27. Throw Out the Cliché

Now let's go after the deadest of deadwood—the cliché. Check your script for those trite phrases, those hackneyed expressions, those stereotyped blurbs that roll off the tongue of most speakers with the greatest of ease. With a snap, too, as if they had the tang of the olive out of the martini—or the onion if you prefer. Speechmakers love them. Put your shoulder to the wheel—plan your work and work your plan—every soldier a potential general—loyal, enthusiastic, whole-hearted cooperation—analyze, organize, deputize. . . .

These are the ones. Speeches are full of them. Let's wrap all of them in heavy paper, tie the bundle securely, and throw it in the ash can. Why? You say you like them, and you feel the audience does too. Look, let's be sensible. You are a fat man, and in this speech you have written, "Like the proverbial stitch in time. . . ." Now that *is* brilliant, but the audience will know that if you had taken a stitch in time you would be wearing a smaller vest. Any one of those tired expressions can sound just as ridiculous. Perhaps you want to use the idea, but say it in your own words.

There are other kinds of material that you should look for in this check. Here are a few:

1. The old stand-bys—the proverbs, the mottoes, the ones that everybody knows
2. The sad expressions that are a part of your business (Business talks are full of them.)
3. The stilted, the out-of-date, the expressions left to us by our grandfathers

4. The popular that has outlived its popularity
5. The clever lines that the audience will sense you did not originate
6. The pep lines that are designed to send the boys out to do or die for dear old whatever, the lines that usually give them a pain.

These are some types of material that should be cut. There are others, of course, but the ones I mention here will send you on a quest for all similar ones you may have in your original writing.

Let's analyze the old stand-bys—the ones that everybody knows and uses. The proverbs, the mottoes, and other such trivia—speech writers always give them a workout. The following story explains what they can do for you. A woman out in the country called a doctor. Her husband had been stricken late at night. When the doctor arrived, the lady was apologetic. "I am sorry I had to call you way out here at this time of night, doctor. But I was so worried."

"Oh, that's okay," the doctor said, "I had to come out this way to see another patient anyway. That lets me kill two birds with one stone."

In my talk "How to Run a Meeting" I use five mottoes to illustrate the effectiveness of one-syllable words. The five are:

A miss is as good as a mile.
A stitch in time saves nine.
A bird in the hand is worth two in the bush.
A new broom sweeps clean.
All's well that ends well.

It is surprising how many times these favorites turn up in speech material. Not as examples, but as bits of wisdom. The speakers often refer to that "stitch in time," to the "new broom," to the "bird in the hand." There are other ways of saying those things, surely. Many times the thought expressed by the motto seems to fit exactly. Well, use the thought, but try to use it in your own words. In your speech you are not trying to be clever. Then why should you write in a motto except to show that cleverness that captivates all your friends? Just a little thought given to any of them will produce a substitute that is more effective, and one that may be much better than the original.

At the start of this chapter I mentioned this old stand-by, "Plan your work and work your plan."

It is a clever play on words, isn't it? But I have heard it used hundreds of times by speakers whose faces lighted up at their own cleverness as they uttered it.

Twenty years ago I heard it, ten years ago, and again just last week. Always when I hear that line I wonder about the speaker. I may have thought of him as the bright-haired boy in his business, but when I hear him speak this old chestnut, I wonder. Has this man's reputation been built up by a press agent? Surely there is some other way to say this same thing. How would he express that thought in a conversation with a friend? He might say, "First, you make a plan. Then you work it."

That expresses the same idea, and if the speaker used those words you would not connect them with the original fluff of cleverness. These words are his. And they are just as strong as, perhaps stronger than, the original quotation. My quarrel here is not with the idea expressed. It is with the manner of expression.

Usually as the chairman introduces you, he puts you on your feet with a cliché. "Without further ado, I give you Mr. . . ." But don't carry on in this vein. The audience will think better of you if you restrain yourself. Here are some of these over-worked expressions that I have noted as speakers said them:

> can't build on sand
> put your shoulder to the wheel
> if the shoe fits
> one for all, all for one
> move to higher ground
> each to his best endeavors
> house of straw
> lick the common enemy
> a picture is worth one thousand words (I have heard this figure quoted at five thousand and ten thousand.)

out of the depths
lost the touch
give no quarter
no stone unturned
fruit of victory
common cause
pull as a team
while the iron is hot
death and taxes
Damon and Pythias
open your mouth and put your foot in it
squeeze play
dwarfs to insignificance
to make a long story short
every hole in the brook
mess of pottage
ball and chain
it behooves us

These are but a few of the many such expressions that clutter up speeches. There are millions like them. If you find any of them in your script, cut them out.

Most of your talks will be business talks, and there is a long list of what I call "sad business expressions." Here are some from my notes:

the business we enjoy
private channels
merit your cooperation
mutual cooperation
executing the plan
hard-working committee
important business leaders
expanding economy
period of prosperity
start from scratch
becoming stale
working as a team
show the light, light the way

demand unfulfilled
performance patterns
management factors
first, second, and third echelons

These are enough to give you an idea of the kind of expressions I mean. If you have any like them in your speech, see what you can do about cutting them out.

Then look for the stilted—the expressions that have come down through the years to us. Let's say you are invited to a lunch at the Waldorf-Astoria Hotel in New York. The man who is taking you says, "This ought to be good. They charged ten bucks apiece for these tickets."

You agree, for ten bucks it should be good. When you get to the Waldorf, you find yourself in a large ballroom. At one end is a head table with three tiers. There are a lot of big names at that table, from business, from government.

As the luncheon starts the room is crowded, every table filled. There must be at least a thousand people, perhaps more. You say this is something. And it is—until the chairman starts speaking. The food is okay, but not worth ten bucks. But you figure that the hotel gets about five, and the sponsoring association the balance. Your host is interesting. So you haven't lost anything until you turn your chair so that you face the head table.

The chairman raps with the gavel. He is an elderly gentleman, with pince-nez, ruddy complexion, hard collar, and white piping on his vest. He is the president of the society, or is substituting for the president. He explains that the mayor was supposed to open the luncheon and welcome the guests but that "he has been unavoidably detained by the pressure of other and more urgent affairs connected with official business."

He doesn't say what he must be thinking, which is "The mayor promised to show but didn't. Instead, he sends some fellow who is third deputy commissioner of this and that, who will now read the mayor's greeting."

But I am talking about stilted speeches. The gentleman, our chairman at the luncheon in the Waldorf, will give it to us. But

everybody else seems to use it too, or almost everybody else. For
example:

the fullest measure
press reports say
a lot of pro and con
afford to be complacent
a full complement of
lend your fullest support
express the preference
with full cognizance
submit to your judgment
instrument of achievement
foundation in justice and righteousness
prolonged era
ample testimony
falls in the same category
striving mightily
afforded an opportunity
for your perusal
prizes will be bestowed
steadily in the vanguard
custom dictates
desirable attributes
has in his possession
desirable ends
the occasion demands

Yes, let's cut all such aged and infirm expressions. With expressions like that you might say, "As the problem becomes more
acute, the solution becomes more urgent." Consider that statement for a second. Speeches are full of such aimless speech. And
there is no reason for it. Most speakers work over their speeches.
Writing them is a chore, a task they worry and fret about. Then
why shouldn't they take the time to show that this work has been
put into the script? When they borrow from the past, they indicate that they have done little thinking about the subject. The use
of such expressions show that the speaker is mentally lazy, that
he can't use his own words to express his thoughts. Certainly you

don't want to give that impression. You want this group to feel that you are an authority.

Then there are a number of expressions that might be called a part of the slang of the day. During the late war the expression "Get there firstest with the mostest" was common in speeches. It was expressive. It was what we wanted our side to do. And so it was good speech material at the time. But speakers still use it. There are many such expressions, for instance:

on the beam	up the creek
hitting on all six	looking like a million
cooking with gas	singing in the rain
eating out of my hand	shooting the works
beating around the bush	shooting fish in a barrel
too little, too late	crying like a baby
the world is your oyster	

These are some of the expressions I have heard in speeches in the last couple of years. So look for them in your script and cut them ruthlessly.

There is another kind of expression that you should leave alone. This is what I call the "clever play on words." It includes these gems, which I have noted from talks:

give rope to hope
aspire, then perspire
battle, but don't prattle
Utopia lies in the first letter

The ideas expressed are good. But they are expressed too cleverly. If you want to use them as they are written, attribute them to some-one else and build a story around them. The line, "give rope to hope" might be the words of some Negro preacher you knew; the second, "aspire, then perspire" to a sales manager who once was your boss; the other, "battle, but don't prattle" to your old army sergeant. But don't use them as they are here. A speaker who says those things can't help giving the impression that he is a stuffed shirt.

If this talk is to be a pep talk, try to avoid the lines that I call "the boss's friends." These are the lines that give the listener the advice on how to succeed. They are the little cousins of the all-time favorite, "Plan your work and work your plan." Here are some that I have noted:

> The wages of idleness is demotion.
> The fellow who feels above his job will always have others above him.
> Let mules do the kicking.
> To get—give.
> There is a difference between living and being alive.
> Use your shoes or let someone else fill them.
> Don't give up—buck up.
> Success is always a conquest.
> Work never hurt anybody—it has helped a large number.
> It is uphill to the top.

I don't have any quarrel with pep talks. They are needed. There comes a time when the club, the employees, or any group needs the needling that only a pep talk can give. But if you are the one selected to give the pep talk, try to forego the worn and threadbare. Use the ideas in these mottoes, proverbs, and snappy sayings, but put them into your own words. By using your own words, you will be more convincing. You will make the audience feel that you believe.

In addition, I am sure that you can do better. Think a while about any of these expressions and you will come up with a thought that is more in line with what you want to say. Use any of the old, and the audience is certain to think of you as a stuffed shirt, or a man with a low-speaking I.Q. Many times I have come away from a meeting with that feeling about a speaker. And I will bet that if I knew the man well, he wouldn't be the man his speech made him out to be.

Once after listening to the speech of the chairman of the board of a big food distributing company, I met a friend in the hall outside the meeting room. "It was a great speech," my friend said.

I nodded, "But what did he say?" I asked.

My friend looked at me for a few seconds, then asked, "Didn't you think it was a good speech?"

I didn't give an inch. "What did he say?" I repeated.

My friend thought for a minute. Then he admitted, "Ed, I can't think of a thing he said."

Now that was exactly the kind of speech the man had given. He had said nothing but he had said it beautifully. His speech was so filled with the charred chestnuts that a man listening and not thinking about what was being said might have thought the speaker was doing a good job. However, a fellow who sat there trying to get something out of the conference was completely disappointed.

I knew a number of men that worked for this food company, so I asked one of them, "What kind of fellow is this chairman of yours?"

"He's a regular fellow, Ed. Why do you ask?"

"I heard him make a speech," I explained.

My friend laughed. "You wouldn't know it was the same guy," he said. "He is not a very good speaker."

Now there wasn't anything wrong about the man's speaking. It was his material and the way it was written. I got the impression that he was a stuffed shirt. I felt that he didn't have a high opinion of his audience for he was giving out blue sky and eyewash, pure and unadulterated. Perhaps he was stuck with the talk. Perhaps he did not want to talk to the group. If so, he should have refused the invitation. For the company that man headed sold something to every person in the room. And wouldn't it be logical for the audience to assume that his products might be just as outmoded as his script?

Keep your talk up to today. Your purpose is to give the group some news, to persuade them to follow your example, to sell them on an idea. Perhaps you have one, or all three, of those objectives. But no matter what your purpose, moth-eaten expressions won't help. Every example I have given in this chapter has been said before, by somebody. Almost by everybody. So why should you say, "Me, too?" There is no reason why you should. You know your stuff, don't you? Okay, then talk as if you do. Use ideas that go back to the year one, if you want to use such ideas. But use them in your words. Let the audience know that you are doing the talking. These are your ideas. Perhaps somebody had these ideas before and expressed them. But you are having them now. So out with the old and on with the new.

I have one more persuasive touch to add to this plea. Next time you hear a speaker get off one of these chestnuts, watch his face as he utters his killer-diller. Note how it lights up as he makes the crack. It is as if a great idea had just struck him. Something big—something colossal—and he is sharing—sharing his big idea with little old you. Why, you, too, should feel the thrill. But instead, it is pain you feel. No, there is nothing wrong with you.

Yes, let's leave the cliché to the other speakers. We—you and I—we use our own words.

I hope this gives you the idea. Get out your pencil and start revising. Here are the suggestions in brief:

1. Cut the old stand-bys—the mottoes, the proverbs, the epigrams, and other such expressions that everybody knows.
2. See if you can get along without those overworked expressions that are a part of your business and so a part of every business talk.
3. Then look for the stilted, the out-of-date, the words and phrases that went well in grandpa's day. Use the ideas but slant them at today.
4. Now look over your popular expressions. A lot of persons today don't know what you mean by "twenty-three, skidoo."
5. Avoid lifting that clever line verbatim from a toastmaster's handbook or a speaker's helper. Lift the idea, but put the thought in your words.
6. If you have any lines that are designed to inspire the group, make sure that they are in your own words.
7. Remember that using any material of the type discussed stamps you as being mentally lazy. You don't want that.

8. Let's say you want to use the idea expressed in a motto, a proverb, or an epigram. Well, study the idea for a few minutes and come up with a way of saying the same thing in your words. Your way will be better speech material.

One thing about the speaker who is afflicted with the cliché is this—he would be the first to condemn its use. Most of us do not realize how we sound when we speak before an audience. It is easy to write the cliché into the script. It isn't so easy to speak it and make it sound real. So throw out all of the ancient and out-dated blurbs. They won't help you make friends.

28. Are You Using Questions?

How many questions have you sprinkled through your script? You should have them. The question can help. There is no need to express every idea in a statement. Statement, statement, statement gets monotonous. A question now and then will add zest. Let's take a series of three statements to illustrate. Suppose I say to you:

> This is the best vacuum cleaner on the market. It has everything to make it the best vacuum cleaner. It has looks, performance, ease of use—everything the user asks for.

That is a string of statements. If I made them before an audience of salesmen that sell cleaners, I might get some argument. Let's say I believe them. I feel that every word is true. I am so convinced of what I say that my manner carries conviction. Let's say I have all of that. Is my paragraph any better when I sprinkle a question or two through it?

> This is the best vacuum cleaner on the market. Why do I say that? Well, it has everything to make it the best vacuum cleaner. It has looks, performance, ease of use—what else can a user ask for?

I have added two questions and the paragraph is improved. Now it will speak better. For with those questions I have done two things. I have emphasized a statement that seemed too strong. I didn't weaken the statement, I strengthened it. And I have brought the audience into the discussion.

Here is how you can use the question in your script:

1. You can use the question to repeat an important point.
2. You can use it to emphasize a statement that needs emphasis.

3. The question varies the pace. You have made a number of statements. You change the formula by asking a question.
4. A question can bring the audience into the discussion.
5. A series of questions can tell you which arguments to hit hardest.
6. A question can tell you how you are doing by observing audience reaction.

There are a number of types of question you can use. First, there is the probing question. It is the kind that the district attorney fires at the witness. "Where were you on the night of March 15th?" That would make a good line in a speech. Although the probing question in the speech might be closer to, "How much income tax did you pay last year?" The probing question can get the member of the audience thinking of his own answer to such a question.

Second, there is the leading question. This one is the kind the salesperson in the store asks. "Would you believe that this suit was marked down from $95?" Your answer to that leads you into a discussion of the suit. In a speech that question might be, "Would you believe that these same politicians are trying to put over that same swindle on you?" The question leads you to agreeing that it is a swindle, and that the politicians are behind it.

Third, there is the committing question. It gets the audience to agree with something. It might be, "Isn't that what we should do?" When a speaker asks a question like that, heads bob up and down all over the house. The listeners are agreeing that it is what they should do.

Fourth, there is the question that inspires action. You ask the audience whether they will do something tonight, or tomorrow; whether they will do it by mail or telephone.

Fifth, there is the hypothetical question. This one sets up an assumption for the purpose of argument. You say, "If you owned fifteen houses for rental, what would be your opinion on this?" Since you don't own one house, this question is hypothetical. Many times the speaker uses such a question to make his point.

There are other types of question that can be used, of course.

But these five show the possibilities. Now let's discuss their usage.

You can use the question for repetition. One way to do this is to repeat the question in slightly different words. Here is a passage taken from a speech to a business group:

> What happens when the public is uninformed? What happens when the public does not know both sides of the story on important issues? What happens when industry neglects to give the people an opportunity to form an intelligent opinion? Here is an example.

If the speaker had handled this part of his speech with statements, this is about how it would sound:

> The public should be informed. It should know both sides of the story on important issues. Industry should give the people an opportunity to form an intelligent opinion. Here is an example of what happens when the public is not informed.

We still have the repetition, but we don't get the same effect we got with the series of questions. The technique of using a series of questions to get repetition is used by most good speakers. If you want repetition of an idea, the question is a useful and effective device.

There is another way that the question can be used for repetition. Let's take the statement on the vacuum cleaner as an example:

> This is the best vacuum cleaner on the market. Now why do I say this is the best vacuum cleaner on the market? I wouldn't make a statement like that if I didn't believe it, would I? I wouldn't make it if I didn't think I could prove it, would I?

Here my questions repeat the statement over and over. They give the repetition, and they add naturalness to the talk. As three statements, those thoughts would be expressed:

> This is the best vacuum cleaner on the market. I believe that it is. I think I can prove that it is.

If I made these three statements, my audience would sit back and say, "Okay, Jack, prove it." When I use the questions, they still want me to prove it, but since I have asked their opinion with those questions, they won't be quite so difficult to convince.

The question can be used to emphasize a statement. Let's take the original statement on the vacuum cleaner and see what the question treatment can do to emphasize the points. Here is the statement:

> This is the best vacuum cleaner on the market. It has everything to make it the best vacuum cleaner. It has looks, performance, ease of use—everything the user asks for.

Now let's see what can be done with questions:

> This is the best vacuum cleaner on the market. It has looks, doesn't it? It gives better performance, doesn't it? It is easier to use, isn't it? Isn't that everything the user asks for? Then why isn't it the best vacuum cleaner on the market?

There are perhaps too many questions in that paragraph, but it illustrates the point. By using the questions, you pound home the reasons why your original statement was right.

One common way to lend emphasis is in the question "Do you gentlemen realize . . . ?"

In the dotted space you give the startling bit of information that is supposed to astound those assembled. Many times a question can be used to emphasize such a point, whereas a statement might go unnoticed.

Not long ago I heard a speaker tell a story about a sales manager. This sales manager was complaining about his salesmen. He said the salesmen were lousy. He admitted that he had hired the men, he had trained them, but still they did not work and produce as they should. He threw all the blame on his salesmen, none on himself.

Later, I heard another speaker tell the same story of this sales manager, but this is how he did it:

> This sales manager said his salesmen were lousy.
> I asked him, "Who hired them?"
> He said, "I did."

"Who trained them?" I went on.

"I did."

"Then, who's lousy?"

Through the use of three questions the facts had been pointed up. Many anecdotes can be built up in the same way. If your anecdote is too short but it makes a good point, add a few questions to build it up.

You can use the question to vary the pace. Let's assume the paragraph is made up wholly of statements. Why not change one of those statements to a question? Suppose your script reads:

> He blames the product, he blames the policies, the advertising, the dealers. Never, not for one minute, does he think of blaming himself.

Let's change the last statement to a question:

> He blames the product, he blames the policies, the advertising, the dealers. Why doesn't he blame himself?

That question gives the speaker a chance to vary his tempo. He speaks—products—policies—advertising—dealers—rapidly—bang, bang, bang. Then we see him pause. He raises his hands. He asks, "Why doesn't he blame himself?" It makes good speech material.

This variety can be had in a number of ways. If you have two long statements, put a short question between them. Make the statement in the long sentence, ask your short question, then answer your question with the second long statement. For example:

> Too many salesmen are inclined to judge the buying power of a prospect by their own. Does that make sense? It doesn't if the salesman happens to be a bit bent financially at the time.

That shows how the question can be used to break up two long statements. As originally written, the two statements read:

> Too many salesmen measure the prospect's buying power by their own. It is particularly disastrous if the salesman might be a bit bent financially at the time.

The question adds variety and picks it up considerably, doesn't it? Your question brings the audience into the discussion. Let's say you have been talking for a number of minutes. Now you ask a question that you want the audience to answer. Immediately the members of the group who have been half awake snap to attention. "What did he ask?" they say.

The question you insert in your talk does not always have that effect, but it does ask for the opinion of the audience. If I am in that audience I feel you are asking me the question. I am flattered. You are no ordinary speaker shouting at me. You are a sensible fellow. You want my opinion. This is interesting.

Your questions bring me into the act. And remember this, every member of that audience wants to get into the act. Many times when I have asked a question, I have had an answer shouted to me. The answer was not expected. If I had made that same point in a statement, no brother would have shouted, "Amen" or "Hallelujah" or "You tell 'em." Statements don't ask for that kind of response. But questions do. If you learn to use the question skillfully, each member of the audience will feel that you are speaking directly to him.

Your questions should be your best indication of the interest of your audience. With a question or two you can find out which of your arguments should be stressed.

If I walk into a hardware store and tell the man I want a saw, he asks, "What kind of saw?"

I say, "Oh, a regular saw."

He asks, "A handsaw?"

I nod.

Now he knows what I want. But if he is good at his trade, he might further ask, "What do you want to cut with it?"

When I tell him, he knows exactly what kind of saw to show me.

You are in much the same position as the hardware man when you rise before an audience. Perhaps this project of yours is important to them. Perhaps you have ten reasons why it is important to them. But while the ten may be equally good to you, that is not true with your audience. Some of those points won't appeal to them at all. With a few questions you can determine which ones arouse interest. When you ask a question that strikes a spark, you can hit that point hard. Lay off the points that seem to have no meaning. Give the others your time and emphasis.

It is well if you can determine this interest before you start to write your talk. Many times that is not possible. After you have given the talk once you will have a better idea of what interests the group. The questions you use during the talk will help you determine that interest.

When you write in the question, you will need some method of getting your question answered. Let's say you have written:

> These tirades against the American free-enterprise system must be answered. Now why do I say that?

You have asked your question, haven't you? Somebody has to answer it. Usually that somebody is you. How will you do it? One way is this:

> These tirades against the American free-enterprise system must be answered. Now, why do I say that? Well. . . .

That gets you off the hook, doesn't it? But you need more than one device. You can't use "well" all through the talk. Another scheme is to use the anecdote:

> These tirades against the American free-enterprise system must be answered. Now why do I say that? The other day, a fellow in Philadelphia answered that question. . . .

Again you are on your way. You can also use all the other interest-building devices that have been covered in this book. You can answer your question with a bit of news out of today's newspaper. It might be out of an editorial. You might use a bit of conversation. You might have one of the audience shout the answer to you. In that case you would act as if the answer were a spontaneous contribution from the member. You would pause, smile at the helper, raise your right hand, point your finger at the man and say, "Mister, you hit the jackpot on that one."

I find in writing scripts I am inclined to use the "well" technique too often in answering my questions. When I go back to revise the script, I change to one of the other devices. That is what I advise you to do. Vary the introduction to your answer in as many ways as you can. The use of one device over and over may get monotonous.

There are a number of reasons why it is good speech technique to change some of the statements in your script to questions. Try a question per paragraph and see how it goes. That may be too many, but try it and see. Make each of the questions short. Don't use the long question. It may be too involved for the listener to grasp. The short and snappy ones are the best. But put in your questions. They improve the speech.

Let's review some of the objectives of your questions:

1. Use the question to get repetition of an important point. Use the same idea a number of times in questions with different wording. Use a statement of the point, then a question.
2. Use the question to emphasize a point that you want to emphasize. It is the old plan of the interlocutor in the minstrel show. The end man asks a question. The interlocutor repeats the question. Thus the question is emphasized in the minds of the audience.
3. The question can vary the pace. You have made a number of statements. Now put the next point in the form of a question.
4. The question always brings the audience into the discussion. When you ask a question you ask the opinion of the members of the group.
5. A question can determine the interest of the audience in the point under discussion. Ask a question and then examine the faces out front. The expressions on the faces will tell you whether or not the point is of any interest to the group.
6. The question will tell you how you are doing. Ask a question and watch those faces for a response. The expressions will tell you how you stand.

29. Other Checks You Might Make

There are many other checks you might make on the manuscript for your speech. Here are a few:

Does It Ring True?

If you listen to the radio announcer, you will know what I mean by this check. He gives his all to the commercial for the laundry soap. If it is half as good as he says it is, the soap will banish the work of washday. But somehow his glowing words leave you cold. You tell yourself, "This guy gets paid for saying this." Have you anything in your script that might bring a similar thought to the listener? Do you claim too much? Perhaps it is the truth, backed by laboratory research, the whole truth, and nothing else. But if the audience doesn't believe it, what then, little man?

Is It in Character?

If you are the boss, does this sound like the boss? If you represent an organization, does your script do a good job of representing the organization? Perhaps you could tell the story about the elephants when you are representing yourself. But can you tell it when you are representing your company or your society?

Does It Do Its Job?

Back in Chap. 2 you were advised to write a synopsis. It might be a good idea to check back to that synopsis and see how close your finished script comes to it. Perhaps in the writing you have shifted objectives. That is okay, but try to look at this opus as an outsider would. Does it do its job?

Are the High Points Spotted Right?

In your speech you have a number of high points—stories, gestures, demonstrations, exhibits. Are they all bunched in the early part of the speech? That is the usual thing. They should be spotted throughout the script so that something to hold interest is always just ahead. If you have the high points bunched, do some shuffling.

Does It Build Up to the End?

Most speeches do not build up as they go along. They start off on a high note and then gradually lose steam. By writing the end first you have assured yourself of a good ending. But how do you build up to that end? The material between the start and the end should build up. Your check may call for a rearrangement, but it is a rearrangement that will pay off in audience interest.

Have You Tested the Material?

Speeches are made up of bits of material—a story here, some gossip there, a bit of news, and what not. While it might be a job to test out the entire speech, it is easy to test parts of it. You can do it in conversation with your wife, with associates in the office. You can have the hired help listen to it. You might even record it on a record, or on wire or tape, play it back, and see how it sounds. Since you have written the speech in units you might test out one of the units as a five-minute speech before your service club. Any testing you can do will give you practice, and it can help the finished result.

Check and check and check—that is one of the secrets of the good speech. If you are not satisfied with one part, keep working on it to see what can be done. Usually, no matter how deadly the subject, you can put life and interest into it if you are willing to put in the licks. So put in that time, that extra work. Make your speech as good as you can.

30. It Isn't Easy, Mister

It isn't easy to write a speech. You hear a good speech and you are inclined to say, "The man is an excellent talker." Perhaps he is. But often that same speaker without his script would have been only fair, perhaps not even good. The script makes the speech, I claim. And the good speech, the one that is alive, is not so much genius on the platform as it is hard work on the script.

As you can see from the chapters in this book, there is much planning involved in writing a speech. After the planning comes the writing and after that the checking. These are the three stages that every speech should go through. The more carefully they are put through that wringer, the better results you will have.

Oh, of course, you can make a speech without going through all this routine. I once had a boss who prided himself on the fact that he could get up without preparation and make a good talk. Time and again I have seen him do it, and he was always good. He was an idea man, that fellow. When he made one of these speeches unprepared, he would stumble along for a time and then he would light into this idea of his. True he hadn't prepared for the speech, but he had given that idea a lot of thought. I believe he was kidding himself when he said he never prepared. He didn't feel that the thinking he did about his idea was speech preparation. But in that thinking he had gone through almost all of the processes that are recommended here for speech preparation. Perhaps his plan was not put on paper, it may be that he never wrote out the presentation, or checked it point by point. But he went through all those processes in his thinking about the speech.

Now that man was different. Most of us are not so gifted. We do things the hard way. To get our speech right we have to put one idea alongside another and then shuffle and reshuffle until we have the best effect. We have to plan, to write, and to check. I hope that the ideas presented here will be helpful.

At the start I said that this was not to be a book on how to make a speech. It isn't—it is all on the writing. But in giving this well-written speech of yours please talk a bit louder than you think necessary, put some enthusiasm into your voice, use some gestures to show that you are alive. Then, too, watch the audience. At the first sign of fatigue, do something. This may be the point to bring up the next story. But don't ignore that first yawn. Look out for your nervous habits, don't fumble with your spectacles or your clothes. Get up on a platform above the audience if you can. They want to see you.

Speaking the piece is the easy part. You will find a number of good books on how to make a speech. But if you have planned it according to these suggestions, written it in line with these directions, and made the checks listed, then your audience is in for a good speech. It will be one that they will enjoy hearing. When it is finished some of the brothers will come up and say, "That was good, Mister." And you will thrill to the greatest satisfaction that a speaker can have. You will know they mean it.

Index